EDINBURGH UNIVERSITY PUBLICATIONS
History, Philosophy & Economics No. 15

the

Struggle

for

Germany

1914 • 1945

Lionel Kochan

EDINBURGH

AT THE UNIVERSITY PRESS

PRINTED IN GREAT BRITAIN
BY R. & R. CLARK, LTD., EDINBURGH

CONTENTS

TO MIRIAM

NOTE ON REFERENCES

The notes and references are printed at the end of the book.
Had they been printed as footnotes to each page they
would have tended to interrupt a text which is meant to be
read as a continuous narrative. In order to minimise the
inconvenience to scholars caused by this arrangement, those
superior figures, in the text, indicating references to
sources have been printed thus [6], those indicating notes
to, and extensions of, the text have been printed with a
macron, thus [8̄].

INTRODUCTION

THE territorial status of Germany has been a problem and a recurrent topic of European diplomacy at various intervals during the last half-century or so—in 1914–17, 1918–19, 1923 and 1941–1945. The aims and the methods of solving this problem have varied enormously; so have their protagonists, from Marshal Foch to Marshal Stalin, from President Poincaré to President Roosevelt. But the theme has remained intact.

This book has as its starting-point the present situation of a divided Germany. It is an attempt to look back to 1914 or thereabouts, and to identify and isolate those factors which have contributed to this development. In this endeavour I have used as much hindsight as possible; I have always attempted to read the past in the light of the present and have therefore been less concerned with motives for actions than with examining the consequences of these motives. It is as true in diplomacy as in personal life—alas!—that there is frequently little correspondence between intentions and their consequences. In the face of this disproportion I have concentrated on what has seemed to me of practical importance, and this was often unforeseen. This does not mean that the development I attempt to trace is not rational—merely that its rationality must be sought elsewhere than in the realm of conscious purpose.

Given this hindsight, the present partition of Germany can best be understood as the result of a contest that has been waged by other powers to secure the allegiance of Germany. This contest has at different times taken within its scope the German social structure, German adhesion to a certain foreign policy and, lastly, the military conquest and occupation of Germany. I would even make so bold as to say that the sequel to the Second World War merely represents the continuation of this deeply embedded contest for Germany. This consideration has led me utterly to reject the supposition that the present partition of Germany is a result of the diplomacy of the war years or of any of the administrative measures taken in the immediate post-war period.

The emphasis on the part played by other powers in the partition of Germany means that German foreign policy as such is relegated to a secondary place. But its contribution to the partition of Germany through its exploitation of Anglo-Russian and Franco-Russian ideological and other differences must be borne constantly in mind.

Partition is not a theme that has engaged the major attention of German historians. Where it is mentioned, the results are often such curiosities as Professor Ritter's description of Allied wartime diplomacy: 'It was agreed systematically to sacrifice Germany to the friendship which Roosevelt and Churchill hoped for from Russia. For her sake it was robbed of its eastern provinces, dismembered into occupation zones, destroyed completely as a power factor, with half of its territory given up to the arbitrariness of the victorious eastern power.'[1]

I attempt, therefore, to fill in a lacuna in the historiography of modern Europe. Through war and peace I follow a recurrent theme of European diplomacy, in a world, moreover, in which the relative weakness of the Tsars was transformed into the relative strength of the Bolsheviks.

This book was begun during my tenure of a Senior Research Fellowship at the London School of Economics, and it was continued and concluded with the aid of research grants from Edinburgh University. To both of these institutions I am correspondingly grateful.

LIONEL KOCHAN

EDINBURGH

CHAPTER I

PROLOGUE IN PETROGRAD

THE approach to total war in 1914 brought with it the approximation to total diplomacy. Certainly, in the mind of several Russian
diplomats, this was no war for limited aims but a war for the
almost complete elimination of the enemy power. Barely had the
crucial battle of the Marne been favourably decided than Sazonov,
the Russian Foreign Minister, put before his allies a plan for the
dismemberment of Germany. It was of such scope as to distribute
almost the entire German territory amongst the Allies. Couched
though Sazonov's outline be in the terms of forgotten dynasties
and vanished kingdoms, it retains authentic significance as the
first plan for the dismemberment of Germany.

'The principal object of the three Allies', Sazonov told the
British and French Ambassadors in Petrograd, 'would be to
break German power and its claim to military and political
domination'. Russia would annex the lower course of the Niemen
and the eastern part of Galicia. It would annex to the kingdom of
Poland eastern Posen, Silesia and the western part of Galicia.
France would recover Alsace-Lorraine and add to it, at its dis-
cretion, a part of Rhenish Prussia and the Palatinate. Belgium
would secure an important territorial addition—its location was
as yet undetermined. Sazonov also proposed to return Schleswig-
Holstein to Denmark and to restore the kingdom of Hanover. He
would reconstitute Austria as a tripartite kingdom, formed of the
Austrian Empire, the kingdom of Bohemia and the kingdom of
Hungary.

These plans, Sazonov emphasised, merely outlined 'a canvas
whose weft is not yet woven'. They had no official importance. But in an aside he whispered to Paléologue, the French
Ambassador, certain words which disclosed the importance he
attached to the maintenance of close contact with the French.[1]
A nod was as good as a wink, all the more so when the Tsar

himself afterwards filled in certain blanks in Sazonov's canvas. The Belgian acquisitions would be 'in the direction of Aix'; and the German colonies would be divided between France and Britain. This drew from Paléologue the rhetorical question: 'alors, ce sera la fin de l'Empire d'Allemagne?'[2]

Not until early in the fatal year 1917 did this Franco-Russian plan for the destruction of German power become in any way official. The scene was a Franco-British-Italian conference in Petrograd; it had as ostensible purpose the better organisation of the Russian war effort and its co-ordination with that of the Western Allies. But the true question was quite different: could the Russian state continue to function at all as a warring body? In these circumstances the French sought to secure from the Tsar —before, as Lloyd George put it, he 'disappeared through the oubliette'[3]—some more definite token of their understanding over Germany. 'In Paris, certain Ministers, and particularly the President of the Republic, had become anxious at not having a written pledge of the Tsar's promise to support our claim to Alsace-Lorraine and to leave us free to organise as we wished the left bank of the Rhine.'[4]

This, then, was one of the first subjects that the French took up at Petrograd.[5] The Franco-Russian negotiations came to fruition in the middle and second half of February. France gave Russia a comprehensive assurance of 'full liberty to determine its western frontiers as it thought fit'. In return, France secured a pledge of Russian support for the restoration of Alsace-Lorraine. The boundaries of Lorraine would take account of strategic necessities and include the iron-ore basin and all the coal-basin of the Saar. 'The remaining territories on the left bank of the Rhine, which at present form part of the German Empire, shall be separated from Germany and freed from any political and economic dependence on Germany; the territories on the left bank of the Rhine which are not incorporated in French territory, shall form an autonomous and neutral state and remain occupied by French troops until the enemy states shall have finally fulfilled all the terms and guarantees stipulated for in the peace treaty.'[6]

The British government was not privy to this exchange of pledges between France and Russia. London, reported Benckendorff, the Russian ambassador in Great Britain, in September

1914, was 'hoping that France would not claim the Rhine line'.[7] Years later Lloyd George could still term the Franco-Russian agreement 'a clandestine and underhanded transaction'.[8] When the Bolsheviks, in the first *élan* of anti-imperialist sentiment, published the text of the transactions, Balfour told the House of Commons that Britain had never expressed approval of the French plan. 'Never did we desire, and never did we encourage the idea that a bit of Germany should be cut off from the parent state and erected into some kind of independent Republic or independent government of some sort on the left bank of the Rhine so as to make a new buffer state between France and Germany.'[9]

In 1917—as at Versailles, somewhat over a year later—it was no part of British policy to re-draw the map of Europe, or indeed the world, in such a way that a French ambassador might rhetorically ask: 'alors, ce sera la fin de l'Empire d'Allemagne?' This was all the more so after the Bolsheviks had seized power in Russia. To the argument that a diminished or partitioned Germany would unduly emphasise French preponderance on the Continent was added the further argument that such a Germany would be the less able to withstand the Bolsheviks and might, indeed, itself turn Bolshevik. None the less, despite opposition on these grounds, the plan of an effete Tsarist Empire, conceived in its last years and confirmed in its dying days, proved of such durability as to form the link between the two world wars. The Germany that was saved by the Russian collapse in the First World War would succumb to a resurgent Russia in the Second.

CHAPTER II

THE RUSSIAN STAKE IN GERMANY

THE night of the Russian revolution, declared Trotsky, in one of his earliest pronouncements on foreign policy, dealt 'a fatal blow' to the war. 'The European governments are no longer concerned with the realisation of their initial aims but with the liquidation of this enterprise with the least possible damage to their rule. It is not possible for either side to think of victory; and the intervention of the working class in this conflict is a factor of immeasurable importance.'[1]

Trotsky seriously over-estimated the rôle of the working class. He had nevertheless put his finger on a distinctive malaise that had been spreading amongst the belligerent powers since the March revolution in Russia. It was this: could the continuation of the war be reconciled with the maintenance of the old régime everywhere in Europe? Might it not be true that war and revolution went hand in hand? By 1917 the slaughter and the carnage and the destruction had reached such overwhelming dimensions that the social system might not be able to withstand the onslaught. One dynasty had gone—the Romanov. Would the House of Hohenzollern survive? The House of Habsburg? The House of Windsor? Where would it end? 'The Russian revolution', House reported to Wilson in August 1917, 'has shown the people their power and has put the fear of God into the hearts of the Imperialists.'[2] This, be it noted, was said of the March revolution, not yet of the Bolshevik seizure of power, a few months later.

In these circumstances, from all points of the political spectrum, voices were raised in favour of some form of negotiated peace. People as far apart as Pope Benedict XV and H. G. Wells were united by their fear of revolution and chaos.

The Papal message of August 1917, for example, though motivated by concern for the patent disintegration of the predominantly Catholic Dual Monarchy, also asked, 'Must the civilised

4

world become nothing but a field of death? And Europe, so glorious and flourishing, is she, as though carried away by a universal madness, to rush into the abyss, and aid in her own suicide?' In more secular terms, Wells, in the spring of 1918 proposed some sort of alliance between himself and like-minded people in Germany as a means to changing Germany and yet avoiding a Soviet revolution.[3] Then there was the Lansdowne peace letter, published in the *Daily Telegraph* of November 29th, 1917. To prolong the war, argued Lord Lansdowne, would 'spell ruin for the civilised world'. He questioned 'the value of the blessings of peace to nations so exhausted that they can scarcely stretch out a hand with which to grasp them'. Was it not opportune that the war 'be brought to a close in time to avert a world-wide catastrophe . . .?'[4]

From *her* side of the fence, Margaret Webb had a month earlier made a confident (but mistaken) prediction: never again would the manual workers 'trust the representatives of the ruling class to dictate foreign and colonial policy without even deigning to discuss it . . . the great majority will press forward . . . to a world based on social equality'. The previous day she had also noted down a highly significant comment made by Lord Milner. He was, said Thomas Jones, a member of Lloyd George's secretariat, 'the most alarmed (of all the members of the War Cabinet) and . . . hankering after peace by agreement with the Hohenzollerns lest worse befall the British and German Junker class alike'.[5]

All these threads were drawn together in a masterly speech by Smuts in Glasgow in May 1918. He advocated a war of limited aims. He rejected the idea of 'the complete smashing of the German army and the German Empire, with a march to Berlin and the dictation of peace there'. An outright victory was impossible for either group of powers 'because it would mean an eternal campaign and the result might well be that the civilisation which they were out to safeguard might itself be jeopardised. It might be that in the end they would have universal bankruptcy of government and the forces of revolution would be let loose. . . .' Therefore, said Smuts, let diplomacy be brought into play, let informal diplomatic contact be made between the combatants with a view to bringing the war to an end.[6]

At the end of 1917 Smuts had himself taken part in diplomatic

talks of this very nature. In a quiet suburb on the outskirts of
Geneva he had talked with Count Mensdorff, an emissary of
Czernin, the Austrian Premier. The British aim was to detach
Austria from Germany, bring about a separate peace with Austria
and make of Austria a balance against Germany. 'The downfall
of Russia', Smuts explained to Mensdorff, 'had created fresh
anxiety for the political future of Europe, and it was feared in
many influential quarters that unless some counter-weight was
established on the Continent to Germany in the place of Russia,
the future peace of Europe might continue to be precarious.' An
Austria able to fulfil this rôle might include, Smuts suggested,
a greater Serbia and a greater Poland in some sort of dependent
relationship.[7]

These conversations had no practical importance. But they
indicate the drift of British thinking towards a policy of balance.
Russia, after the Bolshevik revolution, was of negligible importance so that Austria must be brought into its place as a counter-
weight to Germany. But this was in December 1917. This was
not the way the war would end. During the course of the next
nine months or so, it was Germany and Austria who would succumb to military defeat whereas Russia, Bolshevik Russia, though
militarily negligible, would show itself to be the bearer of a far
from negligible revolutionary message. Not the Boche but the
Bolshie was now the enemy. Better peace with the Hohenzollerns,
Milner had anticipated, 'lest worse befall the British and German
Junker class alike'. There was here a clear and common interest
in thwarting the further spread of Bolshevism. Thus, with the
ending of the war, the contest for Germany as the most important
stake in the impending struggle between *status quo* and revolution took on a truly world-historical significance. The Armistice
itself represented not only the end of the war, but also a phase in
the Allied struggle for Germany and against Bolshevism, both
in Russia and elsewhere.

II

Before taking Allied policy in Germany any further, let us first
consider what it was up against; for what was clear to the Allies
was no less clear to the Bolsheviks. They too, from the first, had
directed their attention to Germany. The hope and expectation

of revolution in Germany had helped to determine the timing of the October upheaval in Petrograd; at Brest-Litovsk, a few months later, the Soviets had tried to spin out the negotiations, playing for time, to enable a German revolution to mature. 'While speaking with Kühlmann and Czernin', said Trotsky, 'we thought of our friends and partisans: Karl Liebknecht and Fritz Adler';[8] and when the moment had come for a Soviet Ambassador to present his credentials to the Imperial German government, he, Adolf Joffe, had done so with the intention of unseating that very government.

Policy towards Germany formed part and parcel of a revolutionary policy pursued wherever the Soviets could bring influence to bear, not only in Europe but in all the colonial territories of the imperialist powers. They combined this with appeals to the belligerents and neutrals for peace—a peace without annexations and indemnities. So far as Soviet Russia itself was concerned, the climax came in February 1919. Chicherin, the Commissar for Foreign Affairs, made a comprehensive and almost humiliating offer of peace terms. Soviet Russia acknowledged its financial obligations towards its Entente creditors; undertook to pay interest on state loans in raw material; offered to lease concessions to Entente capitalists; and even to make territorial concessions, involving the occupation of areas forming part of the former Russian Empire by armies drawing their support from the Entente. If this were all agreed to, Russia would then pledge itself not to intervene in the internal affairs of other powers.[9]

No response came. On the contrary, the hostility with which the Soviets regarded the bourgeois powers was fully reciprocated. At the end of 1917 a Franco-British agreement had allocated to France spheres of interest in Bessarabia, the Ukraine, the Crimea; and to Britain the Cossack lands, the Caucasus, Armenia, Georgia and Kurdistan. During 1918 corresponding positions were being taken up. American troops were disembarking in Siberia, British troops in Archangel and Baku, and French troops in Odessa. Almost at the very end of the war, on October 27th, 1918, Clemenceau was writing to General Franchet d'Espérey, Commander of the French forces in south-east Europe, of the plan 'that it would be appropriate to adopt in Russia, not only in order to continue the struggle against the Central Powers but also to bring about the economic encirclement of Bolshevism and provoke its fall'.[10]

(At this moment Lenin feared the onset of a major crisis. The defeat of Germany had untied the hands of the Entente. The way would be clear for the Entente to invade Russia. He envisaged an advance by Franchet d'Espérey into the Ukraine by way of Hungary and Rumania.[11] In this menacing situation Lenin eagerly looked to the Western revolutionary movement for salvation—to Germany, first and foremost. The Russian proletariat, he wrote on October 4th, is prepared 'to exert all its efforts to help the German workers, who are faced with the most severe trials, the most severe transition from slavery to freedom, the most tenacious struggle both with their own and with British imperialism'.[12] Utopian hopes ran highest at the moment of desolation. A few weeks later Lenin saw in Germany no longer 'a mighty empire' but 'a rotting tree'. He distinguished two trends in German thought and policy. The first urged—'let us hang on till spring'; the second saw 'its principal salvation in England and France and turns all its attention towards reaching an agreement with France and England against the Bolsheviks'. Lenin concluded that the Soviet Republic stood before two stark contrasts —'we were never so near to the international proletariat revolution as we are now; and secondly, we were never in a more dangerous position than we are now'. In resolving this contradiction the German revolution had a paramount part to play. The 'German link' was the most important in the chain of the international revolution 'because the German revolution has already matured and on it depends more than anything the success of the world revolution'.[13]

From now on the Russians gave all possible support to what was thought to be an impending upheaval in Germany. 'Time is pressing. The moment has come. There can be no more waiting', declared Chicherin in an open letter to the German workers.[14] The Soviets' help, in actual fact, amounted to very little. They sent greetings to Liebknecht, the German Spartacist, on his release from prison;[15] they assembled wagon-loads of grain for transport to a Germany suffering under the Allied blockade; moral support came in the form of *Pravda*'s headlines of Novem-

ber 1st: 'The world revolution has begun. . . . Nothing can hold up the iron tread of revolution'; and in December the Soviets sent a delegation of leading Bolsheviks—Joffe, Rakovsky, Bukharin, Ignatoff and Radek—to attend the first All-German Congress of Soviets.[16]

All this, however, could not create in Berlin the reality of the wave of the future. In Moscow it all looked so convincing. Defeat, dynastic and social collapse, and mutiny had released profound tensions throughout Europe. Who could foresee that they would produce no more than ephemeral Soviet Republics in Hungary and Bavaria? On November 9th Liebknecht spoke to the crowd from the balcony of the *Reichstag* and hurled a greeting to 'our Russian comrades'. His words had very little resonance in Germany. Two months later he himself, and also Rosa Luxemburg, were dead—killed by the proto-fascists of the German counter-revolution. The Spartacist group was a tiny hunted minority, with no access to the masses. Not until the end of 1920 did a mass German Communist Party come into existence with more than 300,000 members and several dozen journals. Until then the Bolsheviks had only the thinnest of thin reeds to lean on. For all that, the Russians had staked out their claim to determine the German future.

III

A Russian historian has posed the question: Why did the Allies in November 1918 not crush Germany entirely? 'The fact is that for the imperialists of the United States and the Entente the problem of the conclusion of the war was indissolubly connected with the problem of suppressing the revolutionary movement both in their own countries and in Germany and primarily with the problem of strangling Soviet Russia, this base and lever of the world revolutionary movement.'[17] This is undoubtedly an exaggeration. But it has its meed of truth. At the time of the drafting of the armistice terms House reported to President Wilson: 'I pointed out [i.e. to Lloyd George and Clemenceau] the danger of bringing about a state of Bolshevism in Germany if the terms of the armistice were made too stiff, and the consequent danger to England, France and Italy. Clemenceau refused to recognise that there was any danger of Bolshevism in France. George admitted

B

it was possible to create such a state of affairs in England, and both agreed that anything might happen in Italy.'[18]

Thus, the terms of the Armistice owed certain of their formulae to the fear inspired by the spread of Bolshevism.[19] This applied with particular force to the territories occupied by the Germans in Eastern Europe. This point came well to the fore in the discussions of the Supreme War Council at Versailles. In Eastern Europe, said House, 'the retreat of the (German) troops would be followed by a Bolshevist régime'.[20] This point was taken up the next day by Balfour, the British Foreign Secretary, who argued that on a German evacuation the countries of Eastern Europe would 'become the prey of Bolshevism. . . . We run a danger', he said, 'of imposing a more harsh régime than the German régime and, despite their hatred of the latter, these regions will perhaps prefer German rule to that imposed upon them by a Bolshevik régime.' To avert this danger he therefore proposed that on withdrawal the German troops leave one-third of their arms in the hands of Allied-designated local authorities 'in order to permit the population to defend itself against all disorders and aggressions'.[21] In the end, the Supreme War Council dropped this idea on the grounds of its impracticability. It accepted in its stead a straightforward proposal from Milner: 'all German troops which are at present in the territories which, before the war, were a part of Russia, Rumania or Turkey, must return within the German frontiers such as they were on August 1st, 1914'.[22] There was no mention of a date for this withdrawal.

Somewhat less than a week later the time came for the Armistice terms to be presented to the German delegation, led by Erzberger; and the two days of Allied-German negotiations, November 8th-10th, marked a further small stage in Allied reliance on the German army as a counter-revolutionary force inside Germany and as the protector of central and western Europe against Bolshevism. The German delegates made great play with the threat that the Armistice terms would not only render Germany defenceless but 'would also deliver Germany up to Bolshevism . . .'.[23] This did not over-impress the Allied delegates. None the less they made two significant concessions. The German delegation accepted the military clauses but jibbed at the surrender of the 30,000 machine-guns that Foch demanded. 'If this were done',

the Germans argued, 'there would not be enough left to fire on the German people, should this become necessary. Germany's internal situation was extremely serious. The country was in revolt, infected with Bolshevism. Order must be maintained.' Foch thereupon reduced the number of machine-guns he demanded from 30,000 to 25,000.[24] Rather a bagatelle, one would think, 5000 machine-guns. But it showed the way the wind was blowing.

Of no less significance was the evolution of Article XII of the Armistice (concerning the withdrawal of the German troops on the eastern front). Erzberger countered Foch's demand on this score with a strong warning: that 'the immediate evacuation of the formerly Russian territories, now occupied by German troops, would sacrifice the local population without defence to the horrors of Bolshevism'. Again the Allies yielded. In its final form Article XII was watered down and only called for the evacuation of the German troops 'as soon as the Allies shall think the moment suitable, having regard to the internal situation in these territories'.[25]

Inside Germany, the Allies had the support of two forces whose strength was certainly shaken but by no means destroyed —the Social-Democrats and, through them, the troops at the disposal of the German General Staff. Scheidemann, one of the six-man Social-Democratic and Independent Social-Democratic Cabinet, from his own point of view echoed Sir Henry Wilson. To the latter, the real danger was not the Boche but Bolshevism;[26] to Scheidemann 'Bolshevism was a greater danger than the Entente'.[27] Hardly had Ebert become Chancellor than he arranged with General Groener, First Quartermaster-General, to use troops to suppress any Bolshevik manifestations, to overthrow the authority of the Workers' and Soldiers' Councils and to restore the prerogatives of the army officer. No wonder Chicherin could talk of 'our bitter enemies—the Scheidemannites'.[28]

This policy applied no less to attempts at thwarting Russian intervention in Germany. The Allied position in Germany required this also. On November 5th, the Germans expelled Joffe on the ground of his interference in German internal affairs (as was indeed the case). To this Lenin replied the following day: 'If the German government is preparing to proclaim a breach of diplomatic relations, then we say that we already know this, that with all their strength they are striving to form an alliance with the Anglo-French imperialists'.[29] Berlin soon confirmed Lenin's diagnosis. On November 19th, Ebert's government refused to admit the Russian delegation to the All-German Congress of Workers' and Soldiers' Councils. A Russian writer comments: 'The fraternal hand extended by the Russian government remained suspended in the air'.[30] This was a traumatic experience and probably does much to explain the later Bolshevik animus against the German Social-Democrats.

Haase, Ebert's colleague as People's Commissar for Foreign Affairs, expounded the motives of this policy to the German Cabinet. 'It appeared', he said 'according to all the reports from our representatives abroad, that the Entente was ready to grant Germany under the present government conciliatory (*entgegen-kommende*) conditions of peace and food supplies. But only so long as Bolshevism did not arise in Germany. It was therefore necessary to repel Russian propaganda and also to live on a friendly footing with the Soviet government. . . . There could be no thought of a closer connection, an alliance for example. That would have made our position *vis-à-vis* the Entente, which could employ against us all the violent methods of the Armistice policy, quite untenable. We therefore even avoided contacts which could be in any way misinterpreted or suspected.'[31] Ebert's record of this meeting includes the comment that should there be any growth of Bolshevism in Germany the Entente would at once intervene 'with all its resources'. He could draw comfort from Kautsky's confidence that the Soviet régime would not survive more than a few weeks longer.[32]

IV

The Treaty of Versailles served in part the same purpose as the Armistice which preceded it. 'Paris cannot be understood without Moscow,' it has been said.[33] Any French hope of detaching the Rhineland in one form or another was quickly scotched by the British and Americans. Of course, the overwhelming intent of Versailles was to prevent Germany from again becoming a threat to peace, so that there was no warrant at all for the hope of the German-Social-Democrats that a milder treaty would flow from an accommodating attitude to Allied policy *vis-à-vis*

Russia. But this still left a certain margin for the use of the treaty as an anti-Bolshevik instrument.[34] Article 433, for example, repeats Article XII of the Armistice agreement and stipulates that the German troops in the Baltic were to continue to remain there 'having regard to the internal situation in these territories'. These troops were intended to carry out a policy defined by Marshal Foch as 'establishing in the Baltic Provinces a barrier against the Bolsheviks'.[35]

In other respects, however, the emphasis had changed from the days when the Supreme War Council had drafted the Armistice. In 1919, it was a question of using the treaty as a legal device to prevent Germany from acquiring any influence in Russia, through the Allied creation of a *cordon sanitaire* of small states; and of barring Russia from exerting any influence in western or central Europe. The extension of German influence eastwards or of Russian influence westwards would have contradicted the aims of the treaty. Thus Articles 116 and 117, 292 and 293 create barriers of one kind or another between Russia and Germany, exclude Germany from any position of influence in eastern Europe and Russia from any such position in central and western Europe. These four articles in general terms oblige Germany to accept the abrogation of the Brest-Litovsk Treaty, to recognise in advance any treaties concluded between the Allies with any present or future governments on Russian territory and reserve to Russia the right to claim reparations from Germany.[36]

These articles were adopted shortly before the treaty was handed over to the Germans. They emerged from what was but a cursory discussion in the Council of Three (Wilson, Clemenceau, Lloyd George). Clemenceau proposed the articles 'in order to prevent Germany colonising Russia' and thereby again becoming 'the most fearful power in Europe'. Such arguments dispersed Wilson's doubt concerning the right of the Western powers to put forward demands on behalf of Russia. The Three also argued that to reserve to Russia the right to claim reparations from Germany might work out favourably should a friendly régime come to power in Russia. Clemenceau said: 'We shall then be able to turn to the Russians and say to them: "Look what we have done for you".' To this Lloyd George commented: '"That can only have good effects."'[37]

Apparent quixotery was in fact a Machiavellian gamble that failed to come off. More, this was a true example of a 'purpose mistook fall'n on the inventor's head'. The gamble did not only fail—it actually helped to bring about the very situation it was intended to prevent—the Treaty of Rapallo.[38] When the German delegates to Versailles saw the Articles referring to Russia they refused to acknowledge 'the right on the part of Russia to demand restoration and recompense from Germany'. The Allied and Associated powers maintained their stand unaltered.[39]

This intransigence concealed a certain weakness in both the diplomatic and military spheres. Already in July 1919 Balfour noted: 'The Powers which, six months ago, were the conquerors of the world, could not, at the present moment, impose their will on an army of 120,000 men'.[40] This was a reference to the Baltic situation. Here the ambiguity inherent in the Allied policy of disarming Germany and simultaneously of using German troops against the Bolsheviks first made itself manifest.

By the end of 1919 this weakness was also evident in the Allies' Russian policy. On December 19th, at an inter-allied conference in London, Clemenceau drew up some sort of balance-sheet. 'Intervention has been tried by every means,' he said, 'men, supplies and money—with the object of setting up a stable government'. No result had been achieved. 'They had tried to help Kolchak with material aid,' but Kolchak had retired 'to the middle of Siberia and his troops were in a deplorable condition.' Next, Clemenceau continued, 'the Allies had believed in Denikin and great efforts had been made in his support by Great Britain and, to some extent, also by France'. But Denikin also was now retiring. Rather than persevere in these unrewarding policies, Clemenceau suggested that the Allies construct, 'as it were, a barbed wire entanglement round Russia in order to prevent her from creating trouble outside, and in order to stop Germany from entering into relations with Russia, whether of a political or military character'. To support Poland would be the best way to achieve this. 'It would be a great mistake if we did not maintain Poland in order to dam up the Russian flood and to provide a check on Germany.'[41]

Why, for good measure, did Clemenceau also not throw in such other White generals as Yudenich, Wrangel and Miller? All had already proved their inability to serve the Allied cause, or were soon to do so. In the end, the conference decided to cut short all further commitments in regard to aid for the anti-Bolshevik forces in Russia, leaving the country 'as it were, within a ring fence'. It decided that a strong Poland served Entente interests; and it committed the Entente to aiding, as circumstances required, the border communities of non-Russian population.[42]

Thus, the Allied failure in Russia at once brought prominently into the foreground the importance of the *cordon sanitaire*.[43] This then was an *ersatz* for the failure to acquire influence in Russia, a further expression of weakness. In any circumstances, no doubt, as a sequel to the Tsarist collapse, the border states would have sought an independent existence. But to hope that they could assume the burden of separating two potentially far more powerful states was chimerical. It was excessively optimistic, for example, to attribute to Poland, which had enjoyed no autonomous existence since the beginning of the eighteenth century, 'un double caractère historique de rempart contre la barbarie russe et de contre-poids à la puissance allemande'. Yet this was the view of an experienced French diplomat.[44]

This chimera did not, of course, at once reveal itself as such. To all appearances it was, in Clemenceau's words, a viable means 'to stop Germany from entering into relations with Russia, whether of a political or military character'. To this end the Entente had also made use of German troops in the Baltic, inserted a number of clauses into the Treaty of Versailles and taken a certain amount of care, though not a great deal, to ensure that Germany did not go Bolshevik. In every respect this policy had successfully denied Bolshevik ambitions in Germany. It had thwarted whatever slight prospect existed of a Soviet Germany that would save isolated Soviet Russia and unleash the world revolution. The battle for Germany's allegiance, both in internal matters and foreign policy had been fairly joined in 1918–19. Victory, thus far, had gone clearly to the Western powers.

v

In 1925 Radek pointed to the wider significance of the situation obtaining at the end of 1919: in Germany the victory of the bourgeoisie over the threat of social upheaval, such as it was, coincided, in Russia, with the victory of the Bolsheviks over the White forces.[45] But at the time no one in Russia and only very few people in Germany deduced from this the possibility of a rapprochement between the two victorious forces. Lenin was as confident as ever of world revolution. The Bolsheviks' international position, he declared in March 1920, 'was never so favourable and victorious as it is now'.[46] The Supreme Council had had to lift the blockade of Soviet Russia and the border states— Esthonia, Latvia and Lithuania had been obliged to conclude peace treaties with Russia.[47] Germany gave him particular confidence. The general strike of the German trade unions, which brought about the collapse of the Kapp Putsch, convinced him 'that the time is not far off when we shall march hand in hand with a German Soviet Government'.[48]

In Germany the situation was somewhat more complex. If there was, at the beginning of 1920, little or no inclination to seek a rapprochement with Soviet Russia, there was equally little inclination to become embroiled in the anti-Bolshevik front. There was, in fact, every inclination to hinder the creation of such a front. In the complex Baltic imbroglio, for example, certain German efforts had as objective the withdrawal of the German troops in such a way that the Russians would be allowed to enter the territories of the new states and no *cordon sanitaire* would ever come into existence. A second plan, in direct contradiction to the first, had envisaged the installation of a White régime in Russia in which Germany would find a willing ally against Versailles and the West.[49]

Also typical was the German refusal to participate in the Allied blockade of Russia. This was imposed by the Supreme Council in August/September 1919.[50] The German government shared the desire to act against the common danger from Bolshevism, the German reply explained, but it could only do so on the basis of an acknowledgment of reciprocal rights. 'It is difficult to admit that these conditions are realised so long as the Allied and Associated Powers consider it possible to proclaim blockade measures against the German coasts and German ships themselves at the very same time that they invite Germany to participate in the Russian blockade.'[51] In the *Reichstag* debate on this topic not one of the party spokesmen—from Social-Democrat to German Nationalist—proposed that Germany align itself with the Western powers.[52]

None of this, of course, amounted to anything resembling a Russo-German rapprochement. But had Germany not acted as it did, such a rapprochement would have been immeasurably more difficult of attainment. Anxiety on this score was vivid in Allied, especially British, circles. It was of the 'highest importance', argued the Army Council in January 1920, that the British Military Mission be retained in Berlin. This would enable its Chief, General Malcolm, to keep in touch with 'German intrigues in Russia and Russian action in Germany'.[53] To the same order of apprehension belong rumours and reports of Germans employed in the Russian armies, of plans for a combined Bolshevik-Spartacist attack on Poland, of the need to keep close watch on Victor Kopp (the Russian representative in Berlin), and of a possible Russo-German agreement concerning chemists and medical stores.[54]

These fears helped to determine the further evolution of British policy vis-à-vis defeated Germany: exercise caution lest governmental or social stability be jeopardised. This concern was primarily British. A more sceptical and perceptive view was that of the French—of Jacques Bainville, for example, to whom the constant German harping on the threat of Bolshevism was pure 'chantage'.[55]

But the British took a more cautious and gullible view. This affected their attitude towards the trial of German war criminals;[56] the supply of raw materials;[57] and the reduction of the *Reichswehr*.[58] The French would argue that Germany required to be treated more sternly; the British, more leniently. Behind this dispute lay the larger reality of the major Anglo-French conflict over the European balance of power. The running controversy on the treatment of Germany can be translated into the differing policies of Britain and France. The first sought to reinforce Germany as a balance to French hegemony; the second to weaken Germany yet further in order to reinforce that very hegemony. For the moment it was the French who called the tune on the Rhine; and it was this that helped to give Lenin his opportunity. He would make a daylight reality of the nightmare that obsessed and haunted the British. This reality would bear the name of Rapallo.

But not just yet. In March 1920 Lenin, as we have seen, was as confident of revolution as ever.[59] But optimism, however profound, could not conceal the continued international isolation of Soviet Russia. In these circumstances Lenin used the Russo-Polish War as a means to give history a push. A period of Polish intransigence towards the Bolsheviks, encouraged by France but somewhat restrained by Britain, culminated in the Polish invasion of Russia. In April 1920 Pilsudski, the Polish Premier, marched eastwards; in May he took Kiev in the Ukraine. Then the tide turned. He had to evacuate Kiev. Soon the River Bug was reached, the rough ethnographical barrier between the Russian Ukraine and Poland proper. There was some dissension on the Russian side as to what to do next. In the end, Lenin's view prevailed—that the Red Army should carry the war into Poland in the hope that the workers of Warsaw would rise, open the way to Western Europe and thus relieve the isolated Bolsheviks in Russia. 'By attacking Poland', Lenin said afterwards, 'we are attacking also the Entente itself; by destroying the Polish Army, we are destroying the Versailles peace upon which rests the system of present international relations. Had Poland become Soviet . . . the Versailles peace would have been crushed and the whole international system forced by the victors on Germany would have collapsed. France would not then have had its buffer separating Germany from Soviet Russia.'[60] No sooner had the Red Army crossed the frontier than Polish Bolsheviks formed a provisional Polish revolutionary government.

To Lloyd George this situation—the Bolsheviks advancing on Warsaw, reaching perhaps the German frontier—was 'the most dangerous that had arisen since 1914'.[61] The Allies rushed a military mission and reinforcements in men and munitions to Warsaw.

In Moscow the Communist International was holding its second congress. Zinoviev, its President, has vividly described the mood. 'In the Hall of Congress hung a large map on which every day the advance of our troops was pin-pointed. And every day the delegates stood with absorbed interest around this map. This was to a certain extent a symbol; the best representatives of the international proletariat followed with absorbed interest —one might almost say with a clutch at their hearts—the advance of our armies. We all realised perfectly, if the war aims set before our armies were achieved, that this would signify an enormous acceleration of the international proletarian revolution. We all understood that on every step forward of our Red Army there literally depended the fate of the international revolution.'[62]

In the end, of course, Warsaw was saved. A resurgence of Polish nationalism, divided counsels among the Bolsheviks, military confusion—all combined to thwart the Russian threat to Poland and to Versailles. 'The ponderous balances', commented Churchill, 'have adjusted themselves to a new decision. Poland, like France, is not to perish, but to live. Europe, her liberties and her glories, are not to succumb to Kaiserism or to Communism.'[63] But when the ponderous balances had found their new position, when the smoke of battle had cleared, when defeated Kaiserism and Communism had slunk away, then there emerged an entirely new visage. There was for the first time the prospect of some sort of stability and harmony between Soviet Russia and the capitalist powers.

Radek, who spent the whole of 1919 in Germany, had first envisaged this possibility. He was at that time the only Bolshevik in close personal touch with conditions in Central Europe. This gave his outlook and analysis a certain coolness and astringency absent from the heady atmosphere of Moscow. His experiences in Germany showed him, for example, that world revolution would take the form of 'disintegration' and not that of an 'explosion'. He foresaw that there would be setbacks to the ultimately successful march of the proletariat. He therefore pointed to the necessity of a *modus vivendi* between Soviet Russia and the capitalist world. Finally, he urged the establishment of full diplomatic and commercial relations between Germany and Soviet Russia.[64]

When Lenin himself first broached this possibility, he was attacked by those unregenerate sufferers from the infantile disease of 'left-wing' Bolshevism, who saw in harmony between the socialist and bourgeois worlds a betrayal of the revolution. To this he somewhere replies that if the Soviet state were to have no relations with the bourgeois world it would have to emigrate to the moon. No bad destination, it may be thought, but no answer to the problem. Lenin needed a policy; and this he founded on what he had observed in Germany during the Russo-Polish war.

It was indeed a strange phenomenon—'as our troops approached Warsaw all Germany began to ferment . . .' said Lenin, 'we saw an unnatural bloc of Black Hundreds and Bolsheviks. There appeared a strange type of reactionary-revolutionary. . . .'[65] 'Everyone in Germany, even the blackest reactionaries and monarchists, said that the Bolsheviks would save us, when they saw the Versailles peace splitting at the seams. . . .'[66] In remarks such as these Lenin emphasised that the salvation of Poland owed nothing to German efforts.

This is, if anything, an understatement. The German Chancellor, Fehrenbach, spoke of people who watched the Soviet advance 'with feverish sympathy'.[67] The Foreign Minister, Dr. Simons, proclaimed German neutrality and this, reported Lord Kilmarnock from Berlin, 'is being used to the full extent in order to prevent military supplies from reaching Poland'.[68] Simons also wrote to Chicherin, almost at the height of the crisis, proposing a restoration of Russo-German diplomatic relations.[69]

For reasons of political sympathy the Danzig dockers refused to trans-ship French arms destined for Poland. The same attitude, but of course for different reasons, clearly prevailed elsewhere.

Lenin, of course, was not alone in discerning in Germany 'reactionary-revolutionaries', or an 'unnatural bloc of Black Hundreds and Bolsheviks'.[70] But the phenomenon was to him of such over-riding importance that it provided the basis of Soviet foreign policy for at least the next decade.

Hitherto, Soviet foreign policy tel quel had not really existed. In 1919, Chicherin wrote, 'we sent fewer notes to governments but more appeals to the working masses'.[71] This phase came to an end in the autumn of 1920. It was then that Lenin took account of the foreign-political developments since the revolution —that the Soviet state had survived, that revolution had not broken out elsewhere, that the Polish campaign had failed but that it had revealed, in Germany, a country deeply hostile to the other capitalist powers.

Lenin addressed himself first and foremost to Germany.

'This country, bound by the Versailles Treaty,' he said, 'finds itself in circumstances that make its existence impossible. And in such a position Germany is naturally pushed into an alliance with Russia. When the Russian troops advanced on Warsaw, all Germany was in a ferment. The alliance with Russia of this country, which is stifled, which is in a position to set in motion gigantic productive forces—all this had as consequence that a political mix-up was produced in Germany: the German reactionaries marched with the Spartacists in sympathy with the Russian Bolsheviks and this is fully understandable for it emerges from economic causes. This forms the basis of our economic position and of all our foreign policy.

'Our foreign policy while we are alone and while the capitalist world is strong consists, on the one hand, in our exploiting contradictions. (To conquer all the imperialist powers would of course be the most desirable thing, but we will not be in a position to do that for a rather long time.) Our existence depends on there existing a radical divergence amongst the imperialist powers on the one hand, and, on the other, that the victory of the Entente and the Versailles Peace have made it impossible for the overwhelming majority of the German nation to live. The Versailles Peace has created a position such that Germany cannot dream of a breathing-space, cannot dream of not being plundered, of not being deprived of the means of life, of her population not being condemned to hunger and starvation. Germany cannot dream of this, and naturally her only means of saving herself is by an alliance with Soviet Russia, whither they are directing their glances. They madly attack Soviet Russia, they hate the Bolsheviks, they shoot their communists like real genuine White Guards. The German bourgeois government madly hates the Bolsheviks but the interests of its international position impel it towards peace with Soviet Russia against its own wish. This, comrades, is the second pillar of our international and foreign policy; to prove to those peoples, conscious of the bourgeois yoke, that there is no salvation for them outside the Soviet Republic. And in so far as the Soviet Republic for three years has withstood the pressure of the imperialists, this speaks of the fact that there is one country in the world—and only one country —that successfully rejects this yoke of imperialism. . . .'[72]

In this way, by lining up Russia behind the German national
struggle against Versailles, Lenin would overcome Soviet diplomatic isolation. He did not invent the division of interest between
Germany and the Western powers—that was already explicit in
Versailles—but he exploited it to the full. He made of this division the basis of Soviet foreign policy, supporting, within certain—as yet undefined—limits the German struggle against the
West. By the same token, Germany was bound to maintain its
neutrality in the struggle of the Western powers against Soviet
Russia, i.e. not to take part in any concerted capitalist front.
This was the bargain that was in the making at the end of 1920.

But Lenin had not foresworn revolution; by opposing Versailles he would also be holding out a beacon of hope to those
oppressed by that self-same imperialist peace. In the event, this
attempt to dance at two weddings at the same time, failed. The
continued absence of revolution made it unviable. The other
arm of Lenin's policy—that of opposition to Versailles—pros-
pered mightily and would soon go a long way to dislodging the
Allied grip on German foreign policy.

It was not so at first. The fact of the Russian defeat in Poland
removed some of the German incentive to come to an understanding with Russia.[73] This did not last long. Early in 1921 negotiations were in progress between Moscow and Berlin. They
concerned such topics as military collaboration between the
Reichswehr and the Red Army, a commercial treaty and the
restoration of full diplomatic relations.[74] In January 1921, Simons
was already telling the *Reichstag* that 'communism as such is
no reason why a German republican and bourgeois government
should not trade with the Soviet government'.[75]

This happy prospect was to some extent retarded by German
reluctance, if not apprehension, at jumping the gun in regard to
Russia. Account had still to be taken of Western policy. On the
other hand, a number of disparate events were tending to out-
weigh this factor. The failure of the Kronstadt revolt, for
example, showed the continued stability of the Soviet state; simi-
larly, the almost simultaneous failure of the 'March Action',
an attempted Communist uprising in Germany, once again exposed the weakness of the German Communist appeal and would
reinforce all those trends in Moscow favourable to a provisional

reconciliation with capitalism. In March also, and this is the most significant of all, there was signed the Anglo-Russian Trade Treaty. This, writes one Russian diplomatist, 'served as a door opening on to the arena of world politics'.[76] The Germans dare not be laggards. In order to catch up with the British, a Russo-German commercial treaty was precipitately signed in Berlin on May 6th, 1921, even although certain textual ambiguities still awaited clarification.[77] The need for haste in a Cabinet crisis overcame all other considerations.

Whence came the crisis? From the demands made on Germany by the Allies. As it happened, the climax of Allied demands in respect of reparations and disarmament was reached in March 1921. There was a vast and significant contrast between the enforcement of the disarmament clauses of the Treaty of Versailles, notwithstanding all the tenderness shown to the *Reichswehr*, and the readiness with which the Russians were prepared to contribute facilities to the re-equipment and training of the new *Reichswehr*. On March 8th, Allied troops occupied the towns of Düsseldorf, Ruhrort and Duisburg as sanction for the German failure to disarm adequately or to meet their reparations obligations; and on May 5th, the London Schedule of Payments demanded that Germany accept the Allied scheme within six days, failing which the area of occupation would be extended to the Ruhr. Next day the Russo-German trade treaty was signed.

Further encouragement in the same sense came with the dénouement to the hotly disputed Upper Silesian question. The Reichstag had accepted the London Schedule of Payments in the hope and expectation that Upper Silesia would remain German, as, indeed, the results of the plebiscite held in March would have indicated. In fact, largely as a result of French pressure, it was partitioned, along lines favourable to Poland, despite British protests. A fierce reply came from Wirth, the new German Chancellor. He stigmatised the partition as a *Diktat*—'not only an injustice against the German people but also a violation of the Treaty of Versailles'.[78] Maltzan, the forceful advocate of a pro-Russian policy, replaced Behrendt, the spokesman of a pro-Polish and less anti-French policy, as head of the Eastern Department of the *Auswärtiges Amt*. This change in personnel was correctly interpreted in France as evidence of a trend towards a Russo-German rapprochement.[79] In the summer of 1921 Wirth and Maltzan were already discussing how to expand the provisional agreement of the previous May into a Russo-German peace treaty, eliminating all reparations claims.[80] The treaty served in fact as 'a transitional phase' on the way to the eventual Treaty of Rapallo, to quote one Russian historian.[81] In the autumn, the unfavourable decision over Upper Silesia naturally accelerated and intensified this movement. When, on November 15th, Krestinski handed to Wirth his credentials as Russian Plenipotentiary, he formally expressed the hope that the framework of the May treaty would be broadened so as to provide for 'the closer collaboration of Russia and Germany'.[82] Good progress was made so that by the winter of 1921/22, a corresponding agreement was more or less ready for signature, 'ziemlich abschlussreif'.[83] Ancillary negotiations covering mining, timber and transport concessions to be operated by German firms on Russian soil were also in progress.[84] But neither side felt it appropriate as yet to proceed to sign a formal treaty. The Soviets wished to retain a free hand for their negotiations with the Western powers. The Germans had no wish to jeopardise the atmosphere of the impending reparations conferences.[85]

The fact is that Russia's relations with the capitalist world had become internationalised, a matter of international and no longer of exclusively British or even German concern. This followed from two distinct developments: the first—an appeal by Chicherin for a conference that would bring about a final settlement between the Soviets and the major capitalist powers; the second—the increasing need felt by those same powers to enter into trading relations with Russia as a means to overcome the post-war economic crisis. This was most acute in the case of Britain.[86]

Lloyd George, therefore, seized most avidly on Chicherin's initiative. Once again, he attempted to include Germany in a joint Western and capitalist bloc to confront the Russians. This repeated the pattern established earlier in the case of the blockade, for example, or the Versailles policy of preventing any independent Russo-German contact. This time he attempted to organise, by way of a consortium or syndicate, an international capitalist approach, including Germany of course, to the question of Russian trade. In December 1921, he informed Rathenau, the German Minister of Reconstruction, of this intention. Rathenau pledged his adhesion and at the subsequent conference at Cannes of the Supreme Council he expressed official German support for the project.[87]

Lloyd George got no further. During the Cannes Conference, the French Premier, Briand, was overthrown by the intransigent Poincaré. This removed any possibility of concerted Anglo-French action, still less any action concerted with Germany.[88] The prospect in Germany looked no happier. Rathenau, now Foreign Minister, was all but isolated in his pro-Western policy, with Maltzan, in a key position in the Foreign Office, an opponent of his political chief over the consortium scheme.[89] Chancellor Wirth also decried the consortium project[90]; so did German heavy industry, apprehensive for the privileged position it hoped to acquire in the Russian market.

Lloyd George could also find no succour in Russia. Here the idea of dealing with a united capitalist world was anathema. It contradicted a basic principle of policy. No opponent of the international consortium was more determined than Chicherin.[91]

This disposition of forces became abundantly clear when the Russian delegation passed through Berlin on its way to Genoa. It had no great expectation that the conference would succeed and hoped to anticipate failure by signing a treaty with Germany that would have effectively prevented the latter from acting in concert with the other capitalist powers. But Rathenau maintained his opposition. He was joined in this by President Ebert. At an eve-of-Genoa meeting between Cabinet and President, the last-named referred to Lloyd George's wish for 'a certain trial period' before the resumption of relations with Russia. That, continued Ebert, 'also influences our relationship to Russia'. Rathenau added that 'Soviet Russia had declared its readiness to enter into a settlement of its economic contacts with Germany. On the other hand, we must not thereby allow ourselves to be drawn into a conflict with the Western Powers.'[92] To Rathenau as to the Russians it was clear that the position of Germany would be crucial to the coming negotiations. Hence

C

the former's reluctance to desert the Western front, which would have entailed breaking up the conference; hence, also, the Russian emphasis on this very act. These remarks of Rathenau, and indeed his whole policy, show an acute and sensitive awareness of the struggle in which Germany was enveloped.

But to Lloyd George, when the actual conference opened a few days later, the central issue erroneously appeared to be the inclusion of Russia in some sort of trading and credit agreement with Great Britain. He did not realise his error until it was too late, when the separate Russo-German Treaty of Rapallo was already signed. What happened was that Lloyd George at first pursued the will-o'-the-wisp of some general agreement with the Russians. In the meantime, however, it became possible for those members of the German delegation who had consistently favoured a treaty with Russia to overcome Rathenau's opposition and also to take advantage of the deadlock that had ensued in the talks between Lloyd George and the Russians.[93]

Rapallo annulled all claims between Russia and Germany, re-established full diplomatic and consular relations between them, and pledged the governments 'to co-operate in a spirit of mutual goodwill in meeting the economic needs of both countries'. This sounds innocuous enough and in full accord with Lenin's description of Soviet policy at the conference. 'We go to Genoa,' he had said, 'not as Communists but as merchants.'[94] But Chicherin and his 'merchants' had in fact stolen a most important march on the West. They had vindicated Lenin's programme of 'exploiting contradictions'. In the specific case of Germany, writes one Russian historian, the Soviet government 'took account of the existence of the most profound antagonism between Germany and the Entente'.[95] In so doing it removed, as it were, Germany from the ranks of capitalism and gave Russia, to quote Chicherin, 'a political *point d'appui* of first-rate importance'. 'The Treaty', he wrote, 'marked the end of the first post-war period of the triumph of the victors'.[96] It also broke the continental hegemony of France.[97] Russia had secured some sort of a partner amongst the capitalist powers. This represented a tremendous accession of strength to the anti-

Versailles forces, to say nothing of the fact that at one blow it did much to disperse the Russian fear of isolation.

It was not to be expected that Western policy would acquiesce in this. It was no part of Western policy to allow Soviet Russia its German *point d'appui*. To frustrate this prospect and to maintain the separation of Germany and Russia had been the Western objective ever since the Armistice. Both Lloyd George and Poincaré were fully cognisant of the threat to their stake in the Versailles system that Rapallo embodied. Both would have agreed with *The Times'* verdict that 'Germany and Bolshevist Russia are leagued together against the Allied signatories (of Versailles)'.[98] This was the heart of the matter—that Rapallo struck at Versailles, at the separation of Russia and Germany that it imposed. Not for nothing did Lloyd George roundly accuse the German delegation at Genoa of 'a violation of the conditions to which Germany pledged herself in entering the Conference'.[99]

But how could the position be restored? How could Germany be won back to the Western fold? Here there was no unanimity. Lloyd George saw in Rapallo the possibility of 'a fierce friendship' and a Russia re-armed by a Germany driven perhaps to despair.[100] Shortly before the assembly of the Genoa Conference, Lloyd George had published his memorandum of March 1919 in which he had argued that a harsh peace treaty might drive Germany into the arms of the Bolsheviks.[101] The signature of the Treaty of Rapallo seemed to vindicate this view. British policy henceforth would therefore argue that Rapallo could best be undermined by removing those obstacles that prevented Germany from throwing in its lot with the West.

Poincaré, on the other hand, took a longer-sighted, indeed, a prophetic view of Rapallo. He saw in it a Pan-German threat against Poland—by those Pan-Germans who were 'on the lookout for an occasion to foment trouble sooner or later in the marches of the east and to re-take by force the Polish regions taken from Germany by the Treaty of Versailles. . . . We have before us a political situation which is of a nature to compromise and perhaps upset the equilibrium of Europe. . . .'[102] '*C'est à l'est de l'Allemagne que se produira l'attaque du Reich*', he wrote to the French Ambassador in London.[103]

Poincaré concluded that the danger could best be averted by a closer and sterner supervision of Germany. But this policy failed. The way then lay clear for the application of the contrary British approach. In neither case, however, was it disputed that the struggle for Germany must be pursued, that Chicherin's foothold in the capitalist world must be dislodged.

CHAPTER III

A WESTERN COUNTER-BLOW

'WE will not get round the occupation of the Ruhr', Rathenau told Gessler, the German Reichswehr Minister, when he returned from the Genoa Conference. 'Nothing will hold Poincaré back. This cigar also we shall have to smoke, whatever damage it does to us.' [1] Eight months later Poincaré made good this anticipation. When the smoke from the 'cigar' had dispersed it became clear that the occupation of the Ruhr constituted in fact a turning-point in the history of post-war Europe. It brought to a climax the Anglo-French conflict over the treatment of Germany and the application of the Treaty of Versailles; it signified the defeat of France and its slow subordination to British policy; it thereby pointed the way to the Treaty of Locarno and the resurgence of Germany; it saw the first emergence of Hitler as a political leader; by disclosing the weakness of German communism, it contributed powerfully to the acceptance of Stalin's doctrine of 'Socialism in one country'; lastly, the Ruhr occupation showed the inability of France, *acting on its own*, to produce any major change in the territorial integrity of Germany. Not for the sake of telegraph poles or sacks of coal did Poincaré go into the Ruhr and sponsor the Rhineland separatist movement but for the sake of extending the French frontier to the Rhine, in one way or another. But this task exceeded France's unaided capacity. This was the lesson of the occupation.

The French failure was due to the decisive support that both Russia and Britain gave to Germany. This combination was not fortuitous, as the Marxists say: it flowed from the part assigned to Germany in the respective foreign policy of each power, either as a matter of hope or as a matter of reality. Thus, before there could be any talk of filling the breach in the capitalist front caused by the German defection at Rapallo, it was first

necessary to ensure the survival of Germany. The immediate
consequences of the occupation of the Ruhr was to bring Britain
and Russia together in the attempt to preserve German territorial integrity. Neither could witness with equanimity the collapse or permanent weakening of Germany. Neither power
could welcome a continent dominated by France. The support
that each gave to Germany was the counterpart to the benefit
that each hoped to gain from a sympathetic Germany, pro-
Russian or pro-British, as the case might be.

Radek and Lord d'Abernon, the British Ambassador in Berlin,
echo each other across the breadth of Europe. They talk a similar language, each from his own point of view. To throttle Germany, Radek argued, would entail 'the destruction of Russia as
a great power, for a Russia which has been weakened to the
utmost by the war could neither have continued as a great power
nor acquired the economic and technical means for her industrial reconstruction unless she had in the existence of Germany
a counter-balance against the supremacy of the Allies'.[2] To
Lord d'Abernon, speaking from *his* point of view, it was 'the
essential interest of England to prevent the breaking up of Germany. . . . Directly Germany breaks up that balance (of power)
disappears; France remains in undisputed military and political
control, based upon her army and her military alliances.'[3] Simi-
larly, the Central Executive Committee of the Russian Communist Party saw in the occupation of the Ruhr the violation of
'the right of the German people to self-determination';[4] and the
British Cabinet argued that it contravened Versailles, that it
'was not a sanction authorised by the Treaty itself'.[5] The ter-
minology is different: the British see French policy as an in-
fringement of Versailles, whereas the Russians see it as a sequel
to the imperialist aims embodied in that treaty. No matter—
there is an unmistakeable identity of aim and hostility.

The accident of geography enabled Russia to take a more
positive part than Britain in supporting Germany. There were
perhaps mixed motives here. The Russian endeavour was primarily to prevent any intervention by outside powers, especially
Poland. This policy would reconcile the divergent aims of pre-
serving German territorial integrity and also of furthering any
possible attempt at revolution by the German Communist Party.

Intervention from outside would clearly cut athwart both objectives.

Even before the French were actually in the Ruhr, Trotsky, Commissar for War, assured the German Ambassador in Moscow that Russia would intervene should Poland attempt to occupy Silesia concurrently with the French occupation of the Ruhr.[6] *Izvestiya* made this threat public a month later—'a Polish attack on Germany at the present moment is a direct blow at Soviet Russia'.[7] Trotsky issued a further warning. 'Germany', he told the *Manchester Guardian*, 'cannot fall on Poland. Consequently the Polish attack would have a purely annexationist and piratical character. And Poland is our neighbour also.' [8] There was certainly no written or contractual Russo-German agreement for joint military action.[9] But it is equally true that the Russians held the ring clear for Germany, inhibiting any Polish move that might tend to weaken resistance to France. In actual fact, it does not seem, despite Polish, and also Czech, sympathy for the French, that either country planned seriously to intervene.[10] But it is undeniable that Russian pressure was a powerful weapon in the German diplomatic armoury.

Later, of course, Russian policy switched over to revolution. This followed the fall of Cuno, the German Chancellor. Stresemann, his successor, reversed Cuno's policy of passive resistance and opened negotiations with the French. Since this seemed to portend the collapse of the Russo-German entente, any Russian inhibitions caused by the effects of a policy of revolution on the German ability to withstand France were rapidly dispersed. But the Russian switch came too late. Zinoviev discovered too late that the German bourgeoisie was not led by Rasputins and that German Social Democracy was far stronger than the Russian variety.[11]

But the abortive policy of revolution was irrelevant by comparison with the earlier phenomenon of a Russo-German association in opposition to the French occupier. Lloyd George's vision of the coming together of the two 'pariahs' of Europe had materialised. 'The Soviet Government', wrote Chicherin, 'appeared before all other governments as the friend of the most oppressed country, Germany, whose very existence was gravely threatened.' [12] It was at this period, declared Bukharin, that

there developed 'the maximum flirtation between the German
bourgeoisie and a state alien to it in its social structure'.[13]
But suitors were working to disrupt this flirtation. They came
from across the Atlantic and across the Channcl. The Ruhr
occupation had so exposed the impossibility of Poincaré's policy
that it now became feasible for the British to follow a basically
different approach. The policy of coercion had failed to domin-
ate Germany. It would yield to a policy based on co-operation.
This was the first result. Second, there came the partial American return to Europe. The first development was signalised in
the depreciation of the franc to one-quarter of its pre-1923 value.
Poincaré's electoral defeat in the spring of 1924 was also sympto-
matic. The second result of the Ruhr fiasco—American invest-
ment in Europe—was exemplified in the Dawes Plan and the
policy of putting Germany back on its financial feet. The justification of Rapallo, argued von Maltzan, the head of the Eastern
Department in the *Auswärtiges Amt*, was that 'it had led to the
Dawes Report . . .'.[14] This is no doubt a simplification, but it
does at least indicate the nature of the fresh phase in the struggle
for Germany, a phase that would be primarily diplomatic.
Hitherto, the Russians had made the running; now, with the
removal, or at least the weakening of the French incubus, it was
possible for the British and the Americans to enter the race on
something like equal terms.

At various moments of tension in Franco-German relations
voices had been raised in Germany calling for a Rhineland pact,
a Franco-German understanding. At the very end of 1922 this
utopian call moved a step nearer reality. Hughes, the American
Secretary of State, proposed a conference of financial experts
who would determine Germany's capacity to pay reparations
and remove this whole problem from the political to the financial
level. The United States, Hughes emphasised, had no wish to
see a 'prostrate' Germany. A German recovery was the *sine
qua non* of European recovery. Cuno, the German Chancellor,
took up this call the very next day. He declared that Germany
needed foreign loans in order to pay reparations and that the
presupposition of such a loan would be the French disavowal of
any coercive measures that might be taken in order to enforce
the payment of reparations. Cuno also proposed a Rhineland

pact forswearing war in the region, a pact to be guaranteed by a great power not interested in the Rhine, i.e. the U.S.A.

Baldwin, the British Premier, took up this cause during the actual period of the occupation. In October 1923 Hughes more specifically proclaimed American willingness to participate in a European economic conference 'for the purpose of considering the question of the capacity of Germany to make reparations payments and an appropriate financial plan for securing such payments'. The Dawes Plan finally resulted from all this. It was adopted by the interested powers in the summer of 1924.

Essentially, the Plan linked the payment of German reparations to the receipt of foreign loans. It provided for an agreed annual schedule of reparations payments, a reorganised bank of issue as a means of safeguarding the stability of the German currency and some degree of international supervision over the new *Reichsbank* and the German railway network. As cover for the bank's requirements the Plan included provision for the raising of a loan of 800 million gold marks, of which the major part was subscribed in the United States. This was the first of numerous foreign loans made to Germany. The whole process vindicated a prognosis made by Stresemann at the end of 1922. 'This policy of solidarity in the fight against Bolshevism,' he had then told the *Reichstag*, 'acts as an inducement to the economic forces of capitalism to co-operate in the reconstruction of Germany and at least to try to prevent her collapse. We ought to be glad of the fact. This is the only way, to my mind, in which we can extricate ourselves from the present situation.' [15]

These financial negotiations passed off smoothly for the most part. But a number of disputed points with the French government disclosed both the weakness of France and the connection between the Dawes Plan and the later Locarno Treaty. Thus, the French argued that in case of German default, any of the Allied powers should have the right to take independent action; and, second, that the authority to establish default should be the Reparations Commission established by Versailles. But this was opposed by the bankers—headed by Thomas W. Lamont of J. P. Morgan—who would have to issue the 800 million gold mark loan. The bankers also argued in favour of an early evacuation of the Ruhr. This was natural enough; the chances of floating an international loan would obviously be seriously jeopardised if the most productive part of Germany were to remain under foreign occupation. In the end a compromise was reached, whereby a German default would be established by the Reparations Commission but only by virtue of a unanimous vote including that of a co-opted American member; and guarantees in case of default would depend on discussion between the Reparations Commission, the German government and the bankers.[16] It is unlikely to be a coincidence that the French evacuated Dortmund, in the Ruhr, a mere ten days after a bankers' conference in London had settled the details of the 800 million mark loan.

Baldwin well described the objectives of the Dawes Plan, from the viewpoint of its sponsors, as the preservation of the civilisation of Western Europe. 'The barriers of Western European civilisation must be made strong and firm', he declared, 'against any subversive onslaught that may come from the East, and there is no surer and no better way of doing that than by carrying out the terms of the Dawes Report and bringing once more that great German market into contact with the markets of the world.'[17]

The further attachment of Germany to the Western powers took place at a political and diplomatic level. The links in this chain were the signature of the Treaty of Locarno between Germany and Britain and France in the autumn of 1925, and German entry into the League of Nations a year later. The first of these provided for an Anglo-Italian guarantee of the Rhine frontier between Germany and France and Germany and Belgium. The latter three states also undertook never to resort to war. Germany freely renounced any claims to Alsace-Lorraine; and the demilitarisation of the Rhineland, in accordance with the Treaty of Versailles, was confirmed. All this would enter into force on Germany's entry into the League of Nations—an essential part of the treaty. Also at Locarno, but *without* forming part of the pact proper, Germany signed arbitration treaties with Czechoslovakia and Poland, and France signed treaties of mutual aid with the same two states. The Anglo-French-German agreement may well be regarded as the diplomatic pendant to the Dawes Plan.[18]

The first politician of importance to encourage German entry into the League was Premier Ramsay MacDonald. He spoke in this sense to the Fifth Assembly of the League of Nations at Geneva in September 1924. At the end of the month Stresemann followed up the British initiative with a circular note to the ten member-states of the Council of the League. He outlined the conditions, all revisionist in tone, under which Germany would be prepared to join the League. He gave special emphasis to the German position in regard to Article 16 of the Covenant: 'so long as the present inequality in armaments consequent upon the disarmament of Germany continues to exist, Germany, unlike other members of the League, will not be in a position to take part in any coercive measures'. This brought the reply that the German application must be unconditional. Thereupon Germany addressed itself to the Secretary-General and again emphasised that, in view of Germany's disarmed condition, 'should international conflicts arise, Germany ought to be at liberty to determine how far she will take part in them'.[19] This preliminary diplomatic sparring on Germany's westward road was accompanied at the end of the year by an Anglo-German commercial treaty based on the principle of the most favoured nation. Early in 1925 an Anglo-German *démarche* proved to be the first step to the eventual Treaty of Locarno. This was a proposal for a Rhineland pact. It emanated in large part from Lord d'Abernon. He had, he writes, 'steadily advocated something of the kind for the last three years'.[20] But a Soviet counter-stroke to Western policy was in the offing. Let us move eastwards.

II

There is a certain similarity between the Locarno Treaty of 1925 and the Munich Agreement of 1938. This has often been noted, both in the East and West.[21] Both treaties embodied the attempt to settle the affairs of Europe by excluding Russia and in opposition to Russia. The result in both cases was identical—within a year Russia had broken free from isolation and come to an agreement with Germany: in 1926 the Berlin Treaty, in 1939 the Ribbentrop-Molotov Pact. We now consider the genesis of the first of these.

Chicherin suffered, as had Bismarck before him, from 'le cauchemar des coalitions'. He followed faithfully the foreign-political principle first enunciated by Lenin—'our foreign policy while we are alone and while the capitalist world is strong consists . . . in our exploiting contradictions'. Thus, even at the purely abstract level, anything that tended to remove contradictions, even though, on a Marxist analysis, such an attempt would be in any event foredoomed to ultimate failure, constituted some sort of a threat to the Soviet diplomatic position.

This applied with a particular force to Germany. True, since Rapallo there had been a notable improvement in Soviet relations with the rest of the world. In 1924 a whole host of European states, including Britain, France, Italy, the Scandinavian countries, Austria, Hungary and Greece, had accorded *de jure* recognition to the Soviet government. But this did not lead to any real broadening of the Soviet Union's international basis. Nowhere did it lead to any approximation, however remote, to the closeness of Russian relations with Germany. As ever—both before and after 1924—the Russians remained tied to Germany. This was reciprocal, of course. But the former suffered from a far greater degree of dependence than the latter. Stresemann could, within certain limits, manœuvre between the United States and Europe and play off the British against the French; there was no such freedom for Chicherin—at best a visit to Warsaw or Paris. It was clear, therefore, that any change in Germany's diplomatic position must infallibly provoke the liveliest Soviet interest and alarm.

The fact of the matter is that the Germany of the twenties took an altogether exceptional place in Soviet foreign relations. Germany was the one capitalist power to maintain friendly relations with Russia. It was therefore not only wholly indispensable to the Soviet policy of preventing a capitalist coalition; also, because of its geographical position, it served as a bloc of friendly territory protecting Russia to the west. This explains why the men in Moscow, who justifiably knew no basic distinction between diplomacy and war, should now, in 1924 and 1925, fiercely oppose Western aims *vis-à-vis* Germany and strive to preserve their protective barrier against any Western encroachment.

It was indicative, for example, of the apprehension prevailing in Moscow that only in 1925 is there belated recognition of the value of German neutrality during the crucial early years of the Soviet régime. 'Much of the confusion that prevailed during the intervention between 1918 and 1920', wrote Radek, 'lay in the fact that the Entente had to transport its men and equipment by sea.'[22] Zinoviev went so far as to confess to the 14th Party Congress in December 1925 that 'the intervention against us did not succeed largely because Germany did not participate in it. . . . The picture might have changed decisively if our enemies had at that time succeeded in drawing Germany on to their side, if Germany had not been neutral, but had played an active part in the struggle against us. . . . We must bear in mind that the Locarno decisions are purely directed at making Germany in certain conditions a participant in future intervention against us.'[23] This was a relatively mild but justifiable statement of the Soviet case. Soviet comment ranged from this extreme to Stalin's view of Locarno as 'a plan for the disposition of forces for war and not for peace'.[24]

The year 1924 opened badly for the Russians. Curiously enough, although the Russian attempt in the latter part of 1923 to foster revolution in Germany had little effect on relations between the two countries, a comparatively minor matter—illegal entry by German police into the premises of the Russian Trade Delegation in Berlin—produced a major storm. From the beginning of May until the end of July there was more or less a breach of normal relations. Krestinski, the Russian Ambassador, left Berlin in protest and Russo-German commercial operations virtually ceased. Russia withdrew from participation in the Cologne Fair and the Leipzig Fur Auction. The branch offices in Leipzig and Hamburg of the Trade Delegation were closed; a railway conference was called off, negotiations with German shippers regarding traffic to the Russian Baltic and Black Sea ports came to grief, import licences were cancelled and discussion of a tariff agreement with Germany was suspended.

This was all small beer compared with the storm provoked by the German adoption of the Dawes Plan. The Soviets knew a hawk from a handsaw, especially where foreign loans were concerned, and feared the worst. The next unfavourable move was the German approach to the League. Then, *pour comble de malheur*, there came the electoral victory of the British Conservatives, through their exploitation of the 'Zinoviev letter'. The new Cabinet contained a high proportion of reactionaries and proven anti-Bolsheviks—Churchill (Chancellor), Lord Birkenhead (India), Amery (Colonies), Joynson-Hicks (Home Office), Lord Balfour (Lord President of the Council). All this led Steklov, the editor of *Izvestiya*, correctly to anticipate a reinforcement of international-reactionary pressure on the U.S.S.R.[25]

There was little in the east to offset these threats apart from a protracted series of Russo-German trade negotiations. These began in the middle of 1923.[26] But they had not made much progress before they were interrupted by the incident involving the premises of the Russian Trade Delegation in Berlin. They were resumed in November 1924. Both Krassin, Commissar of Foreign Trade, and Count Brockdorff-Rantzau attended the opening ceremonies.[27] Their presence at this largely ceremonial occasion may perhaps have been intended to serve as a counter-demonstration to the German rapprochement with the Western powers; for although Brockdorff-Rantzau was a diplomat of the old school who detested the public-relations aspect of modern diplomacy and preferred to work *dans les coulisses*,[28] he was also one of the numerous right-wing Germans who bitterly opposed Stresemann's Western orientation.

On the diplomatic front, in the meantime, the Soviets were preparing to launch a strong offensive. Chicherin initiated the attack on September 21st, 1924—a week before the German note to the members of the League Council. He sent a more or less open letter to Professor Ludwig Stein, a noted Berlin journalist. German entry into the League, Chicherin argued, would signify 'a capitulation, a going to Canossa'. What, after all, did the League represent but 'an international guarantee and an association of existing frontiers, in particular the Versailles frontiers, raised to the heights of a system?' 'The League of Nations is a league of victors . . .' he warned. 'By entering the League Germany joins a definite coalition, Germany thereby becomes a satellite, renounces its own political line, subordinates its policy to that of a coalition. German policy thereby comes into conflict with the Rapallo policy. Against its own

wish, through the power of facts, Germany will be drawn into
such combinations and actions as will bring it into conflict with
us. . . . Germany itself will sink into becoming a factor in the
power-policy of the Entente States.'[29]

This letter contains *in nuce* all the arguments that the Russians would ever be able to bring forward to combat the new
German pro-Western line. This would be their unvarying
theme. At times it would receive additional strength from a denunciation of the effects of the Dawes Plan—that Germany, for
example, had paid for internal stability with the loss 'of all
economic and a degree of political independence. . . . The
international control exercised over the basic branches of German economic life by the so-called Dawes Plan must be strongly
reflected in the independence of German foreign policy.'[30] From
this it could further be argued that the German road to freedom
lay through a closer relationship with the Soviet government;
the Russian economy offered 'a vast market' for German industry in return for which Russia could supply Germany with
raw materials, grain and meat.[31]

There was, of course, a certain amount of truth in the Russian
interpretation of Western policy. The Dawes Plan *did* presup-
pose, as Stresemann himself acknowledged, the conclusion of a
security pact in the West; and German membership of the
League *was* intended, as will be shown below, to be a means
whereby pressure might be exerted on German foreign policy,
and to make Germany, as Zinoviev had said, 'in certain conditions a participant in future intervention against us'.

Soviet diplomacy did not confine itself to denunciation. On
the contrary, at the end of 1924 a constructive plan was produced to foil and parry the efforts of the Western powers *vis-à-
vis* Germany. There was at first talk of a joint Russo-German
understanding with a view to putting pressure on Poland and
perhaps even 'pushing Poland back to its ethnographic frontiers'.[32] This phase soon passed, to give way to a broader approach. Chicherin offered Germany a neutrality pact. A *démarche*
of this type had been the subject of rumour in the summer of
1924, at a time when Chicherin was taking the cure at Wiesbaden. He is said to have met there with certain leaders of the
German National Party, which was amongst the most vigorous

opponents of Stresemann's pro-Western policy, and to have discussed with them such a pact.[33]

Be that as it may, the Russian project took on authentic status at the end of December that year. The supreme object was to prevent the accession of Germany to the League. To this end the Soviet government proposed that the two countries bind themselves 'not to enter into any political or economic alliances or agreements with third parties directed against the other'. This was the heart and soul of the proposed pact. As for the League, Chicherin thought this could ideally be met by the joint entry of Germany and Russia or by a joint agreement to send observers to Geneva. Chicherin also undertook to bind Russia not to conclude with France any anti-German agreement, provided that Germany accepted a reciprocal pledge vis-à-vis England. 'We shall do nothing with Herbette if you do nothing with Chamberlain.' [34]

The model here was the type of treaty that Russia concluded with Turkey in December 1925. This bound each signatory 'not to participate in any union or agreement of a political nature with one or several third parties directed against the other contracting party . . . and not to participate in any hostile act on the part of one or several powers directed against the other contracting party'. Rakovsky, at one time Soviet Ambassador to Paris and London, has given an interesting exegesis of its intent. His analysis recalls, not surprisingly, the substance of the criticism made by traditionalist conservative thought of the League—that the sanctions clauses would tend to extend the scope of any hostilities once war had broken out. 'This treaty' (i.e. this Russo-Turkish treaty), Rakovsky writes, 'has this pre-eminence over the protocol on non-aggression embodied in the League of Nations in that it in no degree affects third parties. Turkey, in relation to us, and ourselves in relation to Turkey are not bound by any Article 16 which would commit us or Turkey to participate in measures of financial or military pressure in the case of an active aggressive policy on the part of this or that state. This is truly a pacifist treaty, in the full sense of the word. This is what we juxtapose to the treaties concluded in the League of Nations or under its aegis.' [35]

Chicherin's offer to Germany of an agreement on these lines

would eventually lead to the Berlin Treaty of April 1926. But
for the moment it produced no affirmative response, or indeed,
any substantial response of any kind from the German government. Ignorance was bliss. In his report to the Central Executive
Committee on March 4th, 1925, Chicherin expressed himself in
modestly confident tones. 'We may be certain', he said, 'that
whatever vacillations there are in German policy—and there
have been, there remain and there will be such vacillations—in
the last resort, Germany, despite everything, will not break
with us . . . the very policy of the Entente issuing from the
Versailles Treaty . . . forces Germany to maintain a policy of
friendly relations with the Soviet Republic.' [36] But supposing
Britain were to attempt to dismantle at least part of Versailles?
What then? Chicherin's confident words were in fact the overture to an intense and fascinating diplomatic struggle.

III

On January 20th and February 9th, 1925, Germany sent secret
notes to Britain and France respectively. These outlined proposals for a security pact and would eventually lead to Locarno.
But the German *démarche* did not at first meet with the unanimous approval of the British Cabinet. Austen Chamberlain, the
Foreign Secretary, initially proposed to deal with the problem
of French security by means of a unilateral Anglo-French defensive alliance. He was overborne by a number of Cabinet colleagues—Balfour, Birkenhead, Curzon and Churchill have been
mentioned—on the ground that a unilateral pact with France
would throw Germany into the arms of Russia.[37] This was also
the view of Lord d'Abernon. From the start, therefore, the
Russian question was prominent. Had 'the war grouping' of the
Allies against Germany been maintained, d'Abernon argued,
Germany would have been 'forced into close alliance with
Russia. . . . No solution of the European problem could be
tolerated by English statesmen which threatened the exclusion
of Germany and left her a prey to Russian wiles and Russian
influence.' [38] Chamberlain himself was less explicit on this score.
He would deny, for example, an accusation by Ramsay Mac-
Donald that he had engineered Locarno 'for the purpose of

D

uniting Western civilisation against Russia'.[39] But he made no
denial of the suggestion that Britain sought a closer Western
association on the part of Germany or a weakening of the
German rapprochement with Russia. He could be less discreet,
however, in a conversation with Baron Moncheur, the Belgian
Ambassador in London. 'I said', he told the latter, 'that Russia
was at present outside Europe. Some day . . . Russia would be
restored and reappear in Europe, not, as now, merely as a
fomentor of discontent and revolutionary disturbance, but as
a Great Power. Before that time came, let us link Germany with
the system of the West. Do not let us hold her perpetually at
arm's length until she turned her back on the West, and turning
East, threw herself into the arms of Russia, so that together
they made an anti-Western block.' [40]

In the matter of Locarno, much separated Briand from Cham-
berlain. But in the matter of Moscow their views were similar.
Shortly after the signature of the Security Pact Briand told the
Revue de Paris: 'les coquetteries des Bolshévistes à l'égard des
Allemands avaient restitué au vieux rêve bismarckien un éclat
nouveau. . . .

'Vous avez, dit-il (i.e. Briand) aux Allemands, le choix entre
deux conceptions: celle de la solidarité avec la communauté
européenne et celle de la complicité avec les Soviets; c'est-à-dire
l'isolement de l'Allemagne du côté occidentale.' But when Russia
came to see the Western powers united, Briand continued,
Russia too would be diverted from 'ses efforts pour dissocier
l'Europe . . . la menace contre les Soviets est si peu dans
l'esprit des pactes signés qu'on se féliciterait au contraire qu'ils
aient eu pour résultat de ramener la Russie vers la collectivité
européenne. . . .' [41]

What does all this add up to? That Locarno, like Versailles,
cannot be understood without Moscow. It went far beyond the
mere aim of re-establishing harmony on the Rhine. Lord d'Abernon, indeed, complained that public opinion concentrated so
much on the Rhine that 'it relegated the vastly more important
problem of the defence of Europe against Asiatic communism
to the category of non-urgent.' [42] It was hoped not only to
undermine Rapallo, and consequently to isolate Russia, but also,
if circumstances warranted, to be in a position to use Western

troops in Eastern Europe, i.e. enjoy transit rights across Germany. German admission to the League of Nations would serve this purpose. This, Chamberlain said, was 'a *sine qua non* of any pact, on which no compromise was possible'.[43] It was this that might have put some teeth into the Security Pact, through the operation of Article 16 of the Covenant.

This Article, it will be recalled, obliged League members 'to take the necessary steps to afford passage through their territory to the forces of any members of the League which are co-operating to protect the Covenant of the League'. The case at issue, present to everyone's mind, was a renewed Russo-Polish conflict.[44] In such an eventuality, assuming Germany's membership of the League, Germany would have been obliged 'to afford passage' to French troops coming to the aid of Poland, France's ally. But this was asking a great deal of Germany; indeed, it was asking too much by half. If Germany, in 1920, at the time of the Russo-Polish war had remained neutral and refused transit rights to the Allied Mission and Allied munitions, then what chance was there that a Germany, stronger relatively and absolutely in 1925, would reverse its policy and *grant* transit rights?

This conflict between Germany and the Western powers was fought out at Locarno itself on October 8th, at the Fourth Session of the Conference. The instructions to the German delegation at Locarno already contained the injunction that the German reservations regarding Article 16, as formulated in the 1924 note to the members of the League Council, must be maintained—Germany must on no account be involved in a Russo-Polish conflict.[45] To this position Stresemann held fast.

There were three possibilities of League action by virtue of Article 16, Stresemann said: direct military participation; indirect military participation through the transit of foreign troops; economic co-operation in sanctions through the rupture of economic relations. He then proceeded to dismiss each possibility in turn, as far as Germany was concerned. The first was impossible because Germany was disarmed; the second equally so, for if Germany permitted the transit of foreign troops it would at once be confronted with 'the greatest internal and external political complications'. As for economic sanctions—and here

Stresemann mentioned the specific case of a renewed Russo-Polish conflict—he argued that were Germany to impose such sanctions against Russia, the result would be a Russian declaration of war. In that case, he continued, 'it was possible that the Russian army would overrun the whole of Germany and Bolshevism would spread as far as the Elbe. At such a moment Germany would have nobody to help her. Her eastern fortifications had been razed and she was defenceless against an attack from the east.'

But this alarmed Briand. 'One could not have one foot in the League and another foot, or at least a toe, in another camp', he argued. Supposing Russia did become aggressive, he said, then Germany would be surrounded by friends who would come to her aid. 'He could not imagine', Briand declared, 'that Germany would wish to give economic aid to a Russian attack on civilisation'.

Chamberlain admitted the weight of Stresemann's arguments. But it seemed to him impossible, he added, 'to enter the League, to claim all the guarantees that it gave, and at the same time to refuse from the start every kind of co-operation, direct and indirect'. He assured Germany that if she were involved in war as a member of the League 'Britain would be obliged to go to her assistance with all her armed forces. Those who had disarmed Germany would be the first to re-arm her.'

All this was to no avail. The Western powers certainly brought Germany into the League. But they had to pay the price of a somewhat meaningless formula to take account of the German objections to the full impact of Article 16. 'Each State Member of the League', it ran, 'is bound to co-operate loyally and effectively in support of the Covenant and in resistance to any act of aggression to an extent which is compatible with its military situation and takes its geographical position into account.' [46]

Even if we now take into account all the loopholes, both in the League and in the structure of the Pact itself, that Locarno left open to German diplomacy and pressure, the Western powers had nevertheless succeeded in removing the obstacles to German association with themselves and thus in weakening German dependence on Rapallo. This was a significant achievement. But a significant price had to be paid for it.

In very general terms, the essence of the Locarno negotiations was to treat Germany as an equal. But this was incompatible with the continued existence of the restrictions imposed
by the Treaty of Versailles. Therefore, these had to go—not
immediately, perhaps, but bit by bit. Furthermore, the Western
powers were requiring of Germany that it risk the alienation of
Russia; and this, as was clear to Lord d'Abernon, for example,
must be made good by 'something equivalent on the Western
frontier. . . . Make the latter substantial and the caravan
moves on.' [47]

Whither did the caravan move on? In a number of different
directions. Although Stresemann was under strong economic
compulsion to associate Germany with the Western powers, he
was determined to secure the highest price possible for his
adherence. 'I see in Locarno', he wrote, 'the preservation of
the Rhineland and the possibility of regaining German land in the
East.' [48] To this the Allies had to agree—the British, at least; the
French, of course, not to the same degree. Any German land
regained in the East could only be at the expense of Poland, the
ally of France. Chamberlain, indeed, had refused to guarantee
the German eastern frontier or the Polish Corridor so that two
types of frontier came into existence—a Franco-German frontier
enjoying the support of the British government and a second
'for which no British government', said Chamberlain, 'ever will
or ever can risk the bones of a British grenadier'. [49] Chamberlain
looked forward to a time when Germany would be able to make
'a friendly arrangement on her own account directly with the
Poles'. [50]

This played directly into Stresemann's hand—although the
'friendly arrangement' he anticipated would no doubt be different from that envisaged by Chamberlain. The two policies, the
British and the German, went well together. The renunciation
of British interest in the area and the German reservations regarding Article 16 enabled Germany to seal off Eastern from
Western Europe and prevent aid reaching Poland from France.
In this encouraging situation, Stresemann defined German
claims as the Corridor with the Netze region, Upper Silesia and
sundry frontier corrections. [51] This was not all. Stresemann also
dreamed of the Anschluss with Austria, the end of reparations,

the end of the occupation of the Rhineland, the return of Danzig and the Saar, and the protection of the German minorities at present living 'under a foreign yoke'.[52]

This programme, of course, far exceeded anything conceived of by Stresemann's Locarno partners. It was, however, no more than a logical extension of the price paid in Locarno in order to bring about a rapprochement between Germany and the West and thereby to isolate Russia.

IV

The Russians did not idly witness the attempted undermining of their sole *point d'appui* amongst the capitalist powers. Until the very moment of the signature of the Locarno Pact, Chicherin and his colleagues put the most intense pressure on Stresemann, in an endeavour to recapture Germany's threatened loss of allegiance. Germany, they argued, was isolating itself from Russia; turning itself into a mere instrument of British policy, putting its neck into a Genevese knot. All to no avail. In the circumstances the Russians again brought forward the neutrality treaty of December 1924. But on April 15th, 1925, Krestinsky was informed that Germany could not conclude a treaty with Russia before concluding one with the Western powers. Such an action, said Stresemann, would constitute 'disloyalty' to the West.[53]

It was not until June that things began to brighten up for the Russians. This, no doubt, owes something to the fact that an entirely new factor had entered the complex—the suggestion of a Russian alignment with Poland and France. This was hinted at in a Russian memorandum;[54] and Litvinov reinforced this impression in a conversation with Stresemann in Berlin on June 13th. Were Germany to become involved in the anti-Russian policy of Britain, the consequence might be, Litvinov said—although he, Litvinov, would regret this—a rapprochement of Russia with France and even with Poland.[55]

Stresemann's slightly more accommodating attitude towards the Soviets from now on also may have been in part due to the French reply to the original German note of February 9th. It mentioned a French guarantee of the treaties to be signed between Germany and its Eastern neighbours. Stresemann found this suggestion 'extraordinarily displeasing' (*unerfreulich*).[56]

Be that as it may, henceforward the Russians began to make some headway. At first they could secure no more than agreement on a preamble that Stresemann suggested might be worked into the trade treaty, or published at some later more suitable date. This preamble would bind both countries 'in the spirit of Rapallo . . . to strive for mutual understanding in lasting friendly contact in all questions of common political or economic interest, with a view to making for the general peace of Europe and to refrain from any action that might endanger this peace'.[57]

Chicherin derided this formula as something that was suited to a 'drinking toast' but not to a 'diplomatic treaty'. He likened it to Goethe's *Bekenntnisse einer schönen Seele*.[58] Any serious negotiations in the East had to await the conclusion of the Western pact, now fast approaching its climax. Chicherin, in the meantime, helped on the good work by a visit to Warsaw on the eve of Locarno. Thence to Berlin where some initial coolness in the atmosphere was dissipated by what Rakovsky called a 'proof of the constancy of Germany's feelings towards us'. This was Stresemann's assent to the signature of the long-delayed Russo-German trade treaty and the announcement of a German loan to Russia of 100 million gold marks.[59] A luncheon given in Chicherin's honour in the Reich Chancellery 'passed off in a very animated mood'. Chicherin, we are told by one of his fellow guests, 'ate and drank without any Communist reserve and made all sorts of pointed remarks. Ambassador Krestinski listened attentively to Prince Bülow's witty and sarcastic stories of his experiences with Russian diplomats of Tsarist days. . . .[60]

There was also a business side to this trip. Once again Stresemann took the opportunity to assure Chicherin that if Germany were to enter the League, it would be the German duty, *inter alia*, not to permit the League to 'develop into an instrument with war against Russia inscribed on its standard. Germany had no intention of allowing itself to be used for this'.

Chicherin took no chances. When Stresemann left for Locarno, he, Chicherin, remained behind in Berlin. Dirksen, the head of the Eastern Department in the *Auswärtiges Amt*, was attached at the last minute to the German party. This was intended to serve as token that due weight would be given to Germany's interests in the East.[61] But Stresemann needed no Russian prodding or goading to secure concessions regarding Article 16. Here he was fighting his own battle as much as Chicherin's. True, Stresemann had far different and more aggressive aims in mind than Chicherin—as the near future would attest. But for the moment Chicherin's opposition gave great strength to Stresemann's dealings in Locarno.[62]

Part of the result was embodied in the interpretation of Article 16 that Stresemann secured. But this did not entirely satisfy Chicherin, even although he now admitted that the offending Article was 'really emasculated'.[63] He insisted on a formal Russo-German treaty despite German reluctance to take this step. Further negotiations took place in Berlin and Moscow in December 1925 and the early months of 1926. They were largely devoted to defining the conditions in which German neutrality would operate *vis-à-vis* Russia. The eventual result was the elaboration of what came to be known as the Berlin Treaty. It was signed in April, 1926.

The four articles of the treaty declared that Rapallo remained the basis of Russo-German relations, that 'the two Governments shall remain in friendly touch in order to promote an understanding with regard to all political and economic questions jointly affecting their two countries', that if either party be attacked the other would remain neutral, and that neither would participate in any economic or financial boycott of the other.

In a protocol consisting of notes exchanged between Stresemann and Krestinsky the former spelt out in some detail how and to what extent German neutrality could and would be preserved despite the entry into the League. Germany, said Stresemann, would 'most energetically' oppose any efforts inside the League directed exclusively against Russia. Second, sanctions against Russia would only be considered if the latter opened hostilities against a third state. But to identify the aggressor would require German consent. Should Germany therefore find this identification 'unjustified', it would not be committed 'to take part in measures of any kind instituted on the authority of Article 16'. Lastly, as a final reassurance to Russia, Stresemann referred to the interpretation of Article 16 given by the Western powers.[64]

The day that this treaty was signed Litvinov delivered a little homily in Moscow. 'If Locarno, as we have always suspected, has as one of its aims the formation of a united anti-Soviet bloc and the isolation of our Union—then in that case it must be acknowledged that the treaty signed today in fact contradicts the spirit of Locarno and we may rejoice that to some extent we have succeeded in extracting from Locarno the anti-Soviet sting.'[65]

Is this a fair statement of the Soviet achievement? Does it not perhaps underestimate the achievement of Chamberlain and Briand? There is no doubt, to begin with, that the Berlin Treaty removed a great deal of the shine from Locarno. This is evident in the distinctly frosty 'welcome' that Chamberlain gave to the Russo-German pact. 'I understand that the Treaty has not yet been concluded,' he told the House of Commons, 'and I have not yet seen the text of any of the Articles, but the German Government have given assurances that the Treaty will contain nothing that conflicts with the Covenant of the League or with the Locarno Agreements. Accepting these assurances, and assuming that the final text of the Treaty completely fulfils them, I see no reason to take exception to it.'[66] Briand was also displeased at the news.[67] A group of French diplomats—Fromageot, Seydoux, Massigli and Corbin—objected to the Berlin Treaty on the grounds that it strengthened the critics of Briand's Locarno policy, strengthened Russia at a time when the country was hard pressed financially and economically, and jeopardised the position of Poland and Czechoslovakia.[68]

The heart of Western concern was the fear that the obligations entered into by Germany vis-à-vis Russia might have the effect of preventing Germany from participating in any united action of the League powers directed against Russia. This was the gravamen of the Western protest as made, for example, by Lampson (of the Foreign Office) and Bertholet (of the Quai d'Orsay) to the German Ambassadors in London and Paris respectively. It seemed to Lampson as though 'Germany had entered into an obligation vis-à-vis Russia which would permanently determine German policy in the League in favour of

Russia'. The German assurance to Russia that German concurrence would be required in any League move to identify Russia
as an aggressor, was seen by Berthelot 'as an assurance to Russia
that Germany would never give its concurrence'. Germany
might be asked, Bertholet said, 'whether it was thinking of with-
holding its agreement should all the other members of the League
Council define Russia as the aggressor'.[69]

These Western fears were undoubtedly justified. But even if
Locarno thus failed to achieve the full effect intended, of mono-
polising German allegiance, it none the less weakened the basis
of the Treaty of Rapallo. Although the Treaty of Rapallo was
reaffirmed in the Treaty of Berlin, it no longer enjoyed the same
status. Previously it had been the sole weapon in the German
diplomatic armoury; now it lost its exclusiveness and had to
share pride of place with Locarno. Rapallo had lost its monopoly
value.

This is the measure of the achievement of Briand and Chamberlain. But was it enough ? It fell far short of the hopes of such
optimists as Lord d'Abernon or Ormsby-Gore, the Colonial
Under-Secretary. The latter saw in Locarno, for example, a
'tremendous' significance. 'It meant that as far as the present
government of Germany was concerned, it was detached from
Russia and was throwing in its lot with the Western powers.' [70]
By this standard Locarno was a failure and such a view shows
little understanding of Stresemann's policy of remaining uncommitted to the Western powers.

There is another sense in which Locarno failed; it did not in
any way encroach on the neutrality of Germany, as newly defined and clarified in the Treaty of Berlin.[71] And this neutral
position was all that the Russians asked of Germany—that it
remain neutral and uncommitted. After Locarno and after Berlin, Germany still remained the vast neutral block of protective
territory, closed and barred to any Western incursion into Eastern Europe.[72] This, the major implication of Rapallo, remained
unaffected. The Western powers had made some slight progress
but had still come off second best in the struggle for Germany.[73]

V

'Rapallo had lost its romantic aureole.' This was Dirksen's verdict on the situation created by the treaties of Locarno and Berlin.[74] Russia and Germany were no longer the pariahs of Europe,
no longer linked by a *Schicksalsgemeinschaft*. These two treaties
would lead to a certain loosening-up of the international atmosphere, and create something of a basis for new allegiances and
alignments. The first result was the beginning of a divergence
between German and Russian policy that later became of growing importance. Germany strove with increasing energy to revise
Versailles, 'to throw the French back from trench to trench' as
Stresemann once phrased it.[75] After Locarno, for example, the
Reichswehr budget for 1925–26 jumped by almost 20 per cent.
as compared with the budget for 1924–25.[76] Also at this time
Stresemann defined the aim of German policy towards Poland
as being 'to delay the final and lasting rehabilitation (*Sanierung*)
of Poland until the country is ripe for a settlement of the frontier
question corresponding to our wishes and until our political
power-position is sufficiently strengthened'. This settlement referred to the Polish Corridor, Danzig, Upper Silesia and certain
parts of Central Silesia.[77]

This contrasts strikingly with the Russian offer to Poland of
a non-aggression pact—a move which provoked the Germans to
protest against this Russian breach of the Berlin Treaty.[78] The
Poles refused the offer, as Moscow had indeed expected. The
Germans took it too seriously. But it was none the less significant
in the context of a Russian policy that soon embraced non-aggression pacts or similar instruments with all Russia's neighbours.
By 1929 this network included the three Baltic States, Poland,
Rumania, Danzig, Persia, Turkey and Afghanistan. 'Neutrality,
Non-Aggression and Moscow', it has been well said, 'were
offered as rival attractions to Arbitration, Security and Locarno.
Non-aggression and a guarantee of benevolent neutrality to the
victim of an unprovoked attack were thus substituted for a
promise of active resistance.' [79] A similar broadening of the
Soviet Union's international position took place in respect of the
League of Nations. Not that Russia joined the League—that 'den
of robbers' as Lenin had once called it. But the Soviet presence

at the World Economic Conference of 1927 and the Preparatory Commission of the Disarmament Conference, both of which were held under the auspices of the League, pointed in the direction of Geneva, or at least towards accommodation to existing realities. In 1930 Stalin summarised Soviet foreign policy in the declaration, 'We do not want a single foot of foreign territory but we will not surrender a single inch of our own territory either, to anyone'.[80]

But Germany in the late twenties was far from being a *status quo* power. Given this fundamental divergence of attitude, it could only be a question of time before it became reflected in policy. Not yet, however. For the moment, the Russo-German working arrangement of the early twenties was continued in the later twenties. It is noteworthy, for example, that there was 'very close contact' between the German and Russian delegations at the World Economic Conference.[81] Here the Russians, with German help, succeeded in securing the adoption of a resolution that welcomed 'the participation of all the countries present, irrespective of differences in their economic systems, as a happy augury for the pacific co-operation of all nations'. This was a blow at Britain, which, on the grounds that the Russian Trading Delegation in London was serving as a base for Russian espionage, had recently broken off diplomatic relations with Russia. Also at Geneva, when Litvinov unfolded his dramatic plan for 'the complete abolition of all armed forces on land, on the sea and in the air', it was only Count Bernstorff, the German delegate, who welcomed the plan. He saw Litvinov as the successor to Woodrow Wilson. The Fourteen Points, Bernstorff reminded his audience, had also stated 'that complete disarmament was necessary, a disarmament which only left states the forces necessary for domestic security'.[82]

The Soviets' working arrangement with Germany came most forcefully to the fore when the breach with Britain was consummated. This came at a critical period—at a time when the Soviet Ambassador in Warsaw was killed and Chiang Kai-shek ejected the Communists from the Kuomintang. This made the bond with Germany all the more important. Germany did not fail Russia. In March 1927, i.e. two months before the Anglo-Russian breach, Chamberlain had complained to Stresemann that German credits to Russia were releasing other funds for propagandist purposes.[83] But opinion in the German Foreign Office, in the spirit of the Berlin Treaty, strictly opposed any taking of sides, sought to moderate Anglo-Russian tension and to mediate between London and Moscow[84]; and when Stresemann met Chamberlain at Geneva he expressly disclaimed any notion of a 'crusade against Russia'—rather unnecessarily, it would seem, since no such plan was in Chamberlain's mind.[85] Even so, this interchange must have helped considerably to alleviate Russian misgivings. Rykov, Chairman of the Council of People's Commissars, told the Fourth Congress of Soviets that in the five years since Rapallo the Soviet Union had had no complaints to make vis-à-vis Germany. 'That policy which was laid down at the time of the Rapallo Treaty has justified itself.'[86]

Despite occasional friction and divergence, the two countries marched hand in hand through the more important of the diplomatic transactions of the period. Was Russia excluded from the original list of invitees to the Kellogg Pact? Then Germany would secure its admittance.[87] Was Litvinov ploughing a lonely furrow at the Preparatory Disarmament Commission? Then Bernstorff was always there to remind the delegates that 'the aim to which the Soviet proposals are directed is identical with that which the Commission ought to hold up as its own aim'.[88] In 1929 the two countries even established an unprecedented Conciliation Commission—unprecedented because it admitted the principle of conciliation as between a proletarian and a bourgeois state. And when the Rhineland was finally evacuated in 1930 it was to the accompaniment of *Die Wacht am Rhein*, in Russian. Litvinov hailed the Allied withdrawal as 'the restoration of the rights of the German people in the Rhineland'.[89]

This duet would not last for ever. At about this time—or perhaps a little earlier—it was beginning to break down. There were two principal reasons for this. The first was the increasingly visible incompatibility between the Soviet *status quo* policy and the rise of German revisionism. The Russians began to realise that it might be a dangerous thing 'to restore the rights of the German people'—in the Rhineland or anywhere else. The second reason was more cogent: there were, in the West, developments in progress the effect of which would be to wrest Germany and Russia apart and thus succeed where Locarno had failed.

CHAPTER IV

THE LONDON-BERLIN AXIS

IN the few years prior to Hitler's assumption of power there was a considerable overlap as between British and German policy in Europe. The British refusal to undertake commitments anywhere but on the Rhine—the defence of the Polish Corridor not being worth the bones of a British grenadier—fitted in excellently well with the claims of German nationalism in this area. This identity extended also to such matters as the evacuation of the Rhineland, the rearmament of Germany and the payment of reparations. These were all matters mentioned by Sir John (later Viscount) Simon to the House of Commons in 1933. Britain, he boasted, had 'led the way in restoring Germany to her position as an equal partner, and in removing the discriminations which pressed upon her'.[1]

This process had begun in 1925 and, in a certain sense, it continued until the spring of 1939. For all this period it was accompanied by a gradual attenuation of the Russo-German link which was at times intended and at others an incidental by-product of British policy. But this distinction is hardly material. The actual events strikingly vindicated certain remarks made by Litvinov to Stresemann in the far-off days of 1925. The Russians, Litvinov had then said, expected Britain to support Germany in those questions that Germany would bring up at the League, such as the Saar and Danzig; for Britain was interested in preventing any further increase in French strength on the Continent. Germany in this way would come to look to Britain for an understanding. But Britain was pursuing an anti-Russian policy and this Anglo-Russian contradiction could lead to disputes in which Germany would be pushed on to the British side.[2]

The quest for an understanding founded on a dismantled Treaty of Versailles proceeded more or less simultaneously on a number of fronts—rearmament, reparations and territorial revision. An important early stage had been Stresemann's threat to Sir Ronald Lindsay, the new British Ambassador in Berlin, that '. . . Germany's whole policy of understanding was at stake if the question of military control were not now done away with. An arrangement must be made in Geneva which would set a fixed date for the ending of military control. Naturally, a formula, for example which said that control would be withdrawn by this or that date, if by then all current questions had been settled, would be unacceptable to us.' [3]

Stresemann had his way a few months later. The Control Commission was withdrawn in January 1927. Its final report, detailing the full extent to which its work had been frustrated, was hushed up, lest it jeopardise the policy and atmosphere of understanding. [4]

The next British move in this pattern concerned the evacuation of the Rhineland. Arthur Henderson, the new Labour Foreign Minister, followed a policy that was intended to be far more amicable to Russia than that of his Conservative predecessors; and he did in fact resume diplomatic relations with Russia after their breach under Chamberlain in 1927. For all that, the mantle of Chamberlain had fallen on Henderson's shoulders—particularly where the evacuation of the Rhineland was concerned. [5]

This took place simultaneously with the acceptance of the Young Plan by Germany. The two were interdependent. The Young Plan was elaborated at The Hague in 1929–30. It marked a perceptible alleviation of reparations payments. The annuities were £35 million less than under the Dawes Plan and international control over such institutions as the Reichsbank and the German railways, originally intended to serve as a guarantee for the payment of the annuities, was totally abolished. Stresemann's price for the acceptance of this scheme was the immediate evacuation of the Rhineland; otherwise he threatened to resign. He could not, he wrote to Briand, inform the German public that more than a year might pass 'before foreign troops leave the last piece of German soil. The impact of such a declaration would be simply shattering for the German public.' [6]

Henderson, while the Young Plan was still being negotiated, had said it should be made 'unmistakeably clear that we are anxious that this [the evacuation of the Rhineland] should take place at the earliest possible moment'.[7]

He was able to begin to redeem this pledge a few months later. It was agreed, following the German acceptance, that Britain, France and Belgium would begin the evacuation in September 1929; that all British and Belgian troops would be withdrawn within the immediately following three months; that French troops would evacuate the Second Zone within the same period; that the French evacuation of the Third Zone would be completed not later than June 1930; and that the German government would refer the Saar question to diplomatic negotiations with the French government. This schedule was adhered to and the whole Rhineland was evacuated five years earlier than provided for in the Treaty of Versailles.[8]

After Stresemann's death in September 1929, Sir Horace Rumbold, the British Ambassador in Berlin, correctly anticipated that his successor, Curtius, would 'increase the *tempo*'.[9] This had already indeed proved to be the case. No sooner was the Rhineland evacuated than Curtius brought up the question of the Saar.[10] At this time Sir Robert (later Lord) Vansittart described future German objectives as the re-establishment of Germany as a world power, involving the acquisition of colonies and mandates; the *Anschluss* with Austria; rearmament 'so as to obtain at least parity with Poland'; and a drastic modification of the German-Polish frontier.[11]

As it happened, however, this prophecy was somewhat premature. It failed to take account of the world economic depression. This led in 1931, first, to President Hoover's proposal for a moratorium on inter-governmental war debts; and, second, to the Lausanne Conference of 1932. It was here, through British mediation and pressure on France, that the decision was taken to cancel all further German reparations in favour of an unreal scheme for a German bond issue, the proceeds of which could be placed at the disposal of those powers to whom reparations were due.

The German delegation, led by von Papen, tried to include in the Lausanne Convention a provision for equality of arms. This failed at the time through French opposition. But at the end of the year a suitable formula was found to take account of

French objections. The British, French and Italian governments assured Neurath, the German Foreign Minister, that 'one of the principles that should guide the Conference on Disarmament should be the grant to Germany . . . of equality of rights in a system that should provide security for all nations'.

This concession by Britain—and to a much lesser extent by France—marked for the time being the culminating point of a policy that had withdrawn the Control Commission, evacuated the Rhineland and virtually cancelled all further reparations. In so doing, this policy had also all but severed the Russo-German link.

II

The Russians gave close eye and ear to German developments. From the beginning of 1929 onwards each move in the changing Anglo-French-German relationship and its effect on German revisionism was carefully noted, and the appropriate dispositions were taken. What they saw was the slow breakdown of the Rapallo policy through the German reconciliation with the West; and the consequent Russian fears had a twofold basis. In a remarkable despatch from Moscow, Viscount Chilston, the British Ambassador, pointed out that the reconciliation between the West and Germany alarmed the Russians 'both because it might finally divert the aims of German foreign policy to eastward expansion, and also because it might obtain for Germany increased sympathy, or at least toleration, for such aims'.[12]

Some slight intimation of this anxiety may be discerned in an article by a certain 'Politicus' in *Mezhdunarodnaya Zhizn*, a monthly journal published by the Russian Foreign Office. 'Politicus' examined 'the paths of German economic expansion' and came to the general conclusion that German imperialism—despite the handicap of a late start in the pre-1914 race for colonies and the subsequent obstacles imposed by Versailles—was once again on the path of expansion. This movement drew added strength from the rationalisation of German production after the inflation. 'Objectively Germany is once again being pushed into an activisation of its foreign policy with the aim of consolidating favourable conditions for the expansion in every way of its industrial exports and for the resumption of the export

E

of capital.' Hence arose German trade treaties with, and large-scale investments in, such territories as Rumania, Bulgaria, Turkey, Persia, South America, Greece, Yugoslavia, China and Siam. 'Politicus' even spoke of a Drang nach Osten—'only of course in other forms'. He ended with the assertion that the principal aim of Germany's 'extremely active' foreign-economic policy was to win back that position in world markets of which the Versailles Treaty had deprived German capital.[13] This had clear political implications to which a Marxist, of all people, could not be insensitive.

At the end of the year Litvinov also showed some awareness of the danger that Russia was incurring. 'Our interests', he told the Central Committee, 'are not in conflict with the efforts of Germany to settle her relations with other countries, but of course only in those cases where this settlement of relations does not draw Germany into anti-Soviet campaigns and does not lead her away from the Rapallo Treaty. . . .' [14]

But this is precisely what was happening. Litvinov's cautious remarks formed the immediate prelude to the threat of what Curtius called 'a radical change of mood' *vis-à-vis* Russia.[15] No wonder *Pravda* and *Izvestiya* both wrote of anti-Soviet moods in the German bourgeoisie, reflecting nervously fears of a change in German policy.[16] The whole situation was again analysed most interestingly in *Mezhdunarodnaya Zhizn* by a certain N. Kornev. His article bore the significant title 'Rapallo Crisis?'

Why, Kornev asked, was the German press playing first violin in the anti-Soviet capitalist concert? He saw the answer chiefly in the 'disillusion with the fact that the great eastern neighbour of Germany had once and for all refused to be its agrarian appendage'. But the industrialisation of Russia by no means threatened Germany. On the contrary, the Russian internal market would, with higher living standards, offer vastly increased opportunities. Kornev saw another cause of the Rapallo crisis in the disparate position of the two partners. There had once been two states threatened by Entente imperialism; but the first was now engaged in the socialisation of its economy whereas the second was developing neo-imperialist tendencies. (Although Kornev did not say this, the contrast between the Soviet *status quo* policy and German nationalism was becoming more and more stark.) Kornev ended with the warning that it was more than ever essential for the Germans 'to cease to look on the U.S.S.R. as the historically pre-ordained agrarian "hinterland" to an industrial Germany'.[17]

In the end the Conciliation Commission, as provided for in the agreement of 1929, met in Berlin and produced an agreed communiqué; and Litvinov duly congratulated Curtius in June 1930 on the allied evacuation of the Rhineland.[18]

But these diplomatic courtesies could not conceal the fact that henceforward Rapallo had entered on its protracted swan-song. Germany was mainly responsible for this. Stresemann's successors slowly discarded his twin policy of avoiding firm commitments to the West and of maintaining contact with Russia. In its stead they jettisoned Rapallo and sought and acquired concessions from the Western powers on this very basis. Both Curtius and Brüning, for example, during the 1930 negotiations in Berlin 'were determined to avoid giving any impression that Germany was, even in the most cautious manner, opting for the East'.[19] Again, when the Berlin Treaty of 1926 was renewed in 1931, Brüning sought desperately to hush up the news. 'The Chancellor feared that on hearing the news of some Russo-German accord, the French government would not feel so disposed to give favourable consideration to the proposals which we intended to put forward.'[20] Yet again—when Litvinov proposed to Brüning at Geneva, where both were present, that the tenth anniversary of Rapallo be celebrated, Brüning did his utmost to soft-pedal the occasion. He feared to 'produce an unfavourable impression on the assembled Western world'.[21] Later in 1932, at the Disarmament Conference, at one time the scene of Russo-German harmony, an open clash developed between the Russian and the German delegations.[22]

The impact of such encounters was deepened, it seems probable, by Russian disquiet at the trend of German internal politics. In July 1931 the British Ambassador in Moscow found Litvinov 'pessimistic about the situation in Germany. . . . He apparently fears some form of Fascist government emerging. . . . I think the Soviet government in their heart of hearts would deprecate serious upheaval in Germany at this moment. . . . Apart from fearing possibility of a strong anti-Soviet

Fascist type of government in Germany, they are not prepared
for a Communist movement on a large scale outside Russia.'[23]
From now on things went from bad to worse for the Russians.
Brüning fell in June 1932. He was followed by Papen, where-
upon Boris Stein, a leading member of the Soviet delegation at
Geneva, commented to a colleague: 'German-Russian friendship is now at an end'.[24] Particular fear was aroused by any plans
for Franco-German rapprochement.[25] The advent of Schleicher's
chancellorship brought a slight breathing space.[26] But when he
in turn gave way to the Hitler-Papen-Hugenberg Cabinet, the
worst Russian fears were realised.[27]

During 1933 it became ever more clear that the Germans had
no further use for Rapallo. True, Hitler attempted to draw a
distinction between his internal and his external policy; and he
even ratified the prolongation of the Berlin Treaty—which
Brüning had forborne from doing. But this did not impress the
Soviets.[28] The Germans, under Hitler, committed themselves
irrevocably and irretrievably to the most extreme of anti-Bolshevik policies. Brüning had sought to achieve success in the
West by keeping Germany's Russian connection out of sight.
Papen had sought to secure French agreement to German rearmament and a revision of Germany's eastern frontier by offering to form a military alliance against the Soviet Union.[29] Hitler
brought this line of policy to its culminating point and would
henceforth secure *his* successes on the basis of a common Western and German hostility to Bolshevism.[30]

On the Soviet side a significant turning-point had come in
the spring of 1931, occasioned by the attempted Austro-German
Customs Union. It produced the French offer to Russia of a
non-aggression pact.[31] Only a few weeks earlier Molotov had
described France as the leading power in the creation of an
anti-Soviet front.[32] But he had also emphasised the Russian
desire for a Franco-Russian non-aggression pact.[33] It may be
assumed that when the French hand was eventually extended,
it was grasped with alacrity. By August 18th, 1931, the pact had
already been initialled.[34] A similar Russo-Polish pact was a far
more significant, protracted and difficult step to take. Even in
1926 when German revisionism was only getting under way, it
had been denounced as a breach of the Berlin Treaty.[35] In 1931,

therefore, with the revisionists in full cry, it was a much more drastic step. Taken it was, however. The Russian decision was made public at the end of November.[36]

A month later Stalin took what was at this time the highly unusual, and perhaps unprecedented, step of giving a foreign writer an interview on current Soviet concerns. He told Emil Ludwig, the German author, that he knew there was 'a certain dissatisfaction and alarm' in Germany provoked by the fear that the Soviet Union might guarantee or sanction the frontiers of Poland. But he reassured them that the pact would contain no such obligation. 'We never have been guarantors for Poland and never shall be, just as Poland never has been, and never will be a guarantor of our frontiers. Our friendly relations with Germany will remain what they have been hitherto. That is my firm conviction.' [37] This was the hub of the matter—the status of the Polish western frontiers. 'What is essential for us', said Brüning, 'is that in the non-aggression pact with Poland a guarantee of the Polish western frontiers, which would be intolerable for us, is not intended by the Soviet Government. . . .'[38] As a further reassurance to the Germans, Litvinov kept Dirksen *au courant* of the Russo-Polish negotiations.[39] The pact with Poland represented a Soviet attempt to ride two horses at the same time—a German and a French.

As this suggests, the Soviets continued to hope against hope. At the end of 1933 and the beginning of 1934, Stalin, Litvinov and Molotov all held out a last hand to Hitler. They emphasised that Russian policy towards Germany was determined by German external and not its internal policy, that the Soviets desired, as always, to maintain friendly relations with Germany, that fascism was no issue to divide the two countries.[40] All spoke to no avail. For the foreseeable future the Soviet policy of maintaining a *point d'appui* in Germany had suffered failure. The Soviet Union was isolated, confronted by a Germany that had aligned itself with the Western powers. This particular phase of the struggle for Germany had ended in a decisive victory for Britain.

III

In our special context, Hitler's assumption of power caused no basic change in the policy of the European powers. None the less, 'the increased *tempo*' which Sir Horace Rumbold had noticed in 1930 did in fact bring considerably nearer the actual partition of Germany. At this very time General v. Seeckt, an early, if not the earliest, supporter of Rapallo and now an opponent of Nazi foreign policy, evoked the memory of the war years—a Germany between two fires. Is this to happen once again, he asked? Is the Polish fleet to threaten our north-west coast and separate us from East Prussia? 'Shall Poland advance to the Oder? Such possibilities assume tangible form if we leave Russia out of our calculations.'[41] A few years later another German military source saw the possibility of South Germany being cut off from the north through the operation of the Franco-Czech alliance.[42]

Seeckt, of course, was envisaging a war limited to the West, against France and Britain. For this purpose a friendly Russia to the German rear was indispensable as a means of bringing pressure to bear on Poland. His forecast of a Poland on the Oder, even if achieved by very different paths, remains remarkable none the less. And it was the first intimation of Nazi foreign policy that inspired it. These consequences, however, lay in the remote future. For the moment the same trends continued to manifest themselves as in the pre-Hitler period but with growing force, i.e. there was an accelerating tendency on the German side to reject Rapallo, an increasing British withdrawal from Europe, expressed in the refusal to undertake any further commitments, and a temporarily deepening trend towards a Russo-French rapprochement, inspired by Russian fear of isolation.

These phenomena and the way they anticipated the future can all be seen operative in the Barthou-Litvinov project in 1934/35 for an Eastern Locarno. This comprehensive project had as its aim the stabilisation of the existing European situation. It provided for a treaty of regional assistance between Poland, Russia, Germany, Czechoslovakia and the Baltic countries; and for a Franco-Russian treaty of mutual aid. The whole was conditional on Russian entry into the League.

But this project failed—not that it ever had much chance of success. 'What particularly appears to us to be impossible', Neurath wrote to Litvinov, 'is to make any political agreements with the Soviet Union affecting our neighbours to the east. For example, an obligation to consult the Soviet government on every political measure affecting the neighbouring states would rob our eastern policy, notably as regards Poland, of all freedom of action.' [43] The Poles also rejected the project. The British attitude was lukewarm in its stipulation 'that it must be quite clear that the United Kingdom was not itself about to undertake any new commitments in Europe. All he [Sir John Simon] proposed His Majesty's government should do would be to recommend the scheme because of the British belief in regional security pacts on the Locarno model and because the scheme came within the framework of the League.' [44] In fact, Simon could only recommend the pact to Germany on the grounds that it averted 'the threatened alternative of a formal Franco-Russian alliance'. Britain, he said, wished to avoid such an alliance 'as being the decisive step towards relapsing into the system of pre-war alliances'.[45]

In the end, all that remained of the Barthou-Litvinov plan for an Eastern Locarno was a Franco-Russian pact of mutual assistance. But it entailed none of the consequences that Simon had feared. Not only did it contain a protocol guarding France against any commitment that might bring it into conflict with Britain; the pact also lacked teeth. The French refused the Russian offer of military conversations which alone could have made the pact into an effective instrument.[46]

In the light of the future, the main theme to emerge from the negotiations for an Eastern Locarno was the reluctance of Britain, and later of France, to be associated with Russia in any opposition to Germany. This was in fact the heyday of the Anglo-German association. Was it a question of bringing Russia into the League? Then there was always Sir John Simon to say: '. . . we should not oppose such an idea, though we shall, as practical people, be in no hurry to be enthusiastic, but would judge by results'.[47] Was it a question of opposition to the reoccupation of the Rhineland? But surely, argued Baldwin, the French 'could be brought to see that a Germany crushed by

France and Russia would be a Communist Germany'.[48] And
during the Spanish civil war it was Baldwin who warned Eden
that 'on no account, French or other, must he bring us in to
fight on the side of the Russians'.[49]

There were differences of course between, say, Baldwin and
Chamberlain, between Chamberlain and Halifax, between Britain and France. Many nuances of response to Nazism existed.
But none was such as to go beyond the framework of accepting
Germany as a partner in the struggle against Bolshevism and in
the isolation of Russia. This acceptance extended to the intro-
duction of conscription in Germany, the Anglo-German Naval
Agreement, the denunciation of Locarno and the occupation
of the Rhineland, the *Anschluss* with Austria and the incorporation of the Sudetenland. These were the highlights in a career
of aggression which was not allowed to alter Western policy.

The pattern of pre-Hitler days continued to operate. Halifax
indeed pointed this out to Hitler in 1937. 'Britons were realists,'
he said, 'and were perhaps more than others convinced that
mistakes had been made in the Treaty of Versailles which had
to be put right.' Halifax then instanced the British rôle in securing the evacuation of the Rhineland before the due date, the
settlement of the reparations problem and the reoccupation of
the Rhineland.[50]

This 'realistic' attitude to Germany depended on an identity,
or at least an overlapping, of views as regards Germany's place
in Europe. Hitler intended to make Germany the hub of the
Western world against the attacks of Bolshevism.[51] This coincided
precisely with Halifax's view. He himself and other governmental colleagues, he told Hitler, 'were fully aware that the
Führer had not only achieved a great deal inside Germany herself, but that, by destroying Communism in his country, he had
barred its road to Western Europe and that Germany therefore
could rightly be regarded as a bulwark of the West against
Bolshevism'.[52] This sympathy for Hitler and hostility to Russia
also expressed itself in opposition to the Franco-Russian
pact.[53]

By extension, the analysis of Germany as the bulwark of the
West made it logical to attribute to Germany the chief rôle in
the actual destruction of Bolshevism. 'The non-Fascist Right

in England and Germany', wrote Sir William Hayter many years later, 'thought that Fascism would do their dirty work for them.'[54] An early essay in this genre came from Lord Lothian. 'You would go through the Russian Army like butter', he encouragingly told General Blomberg, the *Reichswehr* Minister, who had earlier spoken cautiously of Russian material and numerical superiority.[55]

This was in 1935. But it was not until the end of 1938 and the beginning of 1939 that such ideas began to appear to be practical politics. Foreign observers in London were now, after Munich, of one mind that Hitler, with British concurrence, would strike eastwards, against Russia. To Raczynski, for example, the Polish Ambassador in London, there was no doubt but that 'a conflict in eastern Europe which threatens in one way or another to embroil Germany and Russia is *universally and subconsciously regarded here as a "lesser evil" capable of deferring the menace to the Empire and its overseas components for a longer period* . . . the Premier officially is particularly careful to avoid doing anything to oppose Germany's designs in the East'.[56] Dirksen, now the German Ambassador in London, reported that 'a further German penetration towards the Ukraine . . . would be accepted. . . . It can be assumed that, in accordance with the basic trend of Chamberlain's policy [authoritative circles] will accept a German expansionist policy in Eastern Europe. In this connection the Polish question recedes into the background as compared with the Ukrainian question. It is expected that the first move for a new order in Eastern Europe will arise out of the Ukrainian question, which would be tackled by Germany and brought to a head.' [57]

Had this German attack come about, it would have crowned the uninterrupted British tendency to look on Germany as an agent of anti-Bolshevik hostility. This policy had first emerged in 1918 and it continued, with varying success, until 1939. Until then, the British and French had in Hitler a collaborator. It was this identity of aim that made of anti-Bolshevism such a powerful weapon in Hitler's hands. 'The Anti-Comintern Pact is no threat to the Soviet Union', Litvinov truly said. 'It is dust in the eyes of the Western democracies.'[58] Deceived as they were, however, the British—until March 1939, that is—could yet find satisfaction in the conviction that the contest for Germany had swung in their favour, that a Germany sympathetic to Western aims had come into existence.

IV

'We do not want to be isolated in international affairs', declared Troyanovsky, the Russian Ambassador, to the American-Russian Chamber of Commerce in New York in early 1938.[59] But the Soviets *were* more or less isolated—as had been the case since 1931 approximately, with Rapallo in a state of collapse and no substitute forthcoming. True, there were the French and Polish non-aggression pacts and later the Russo-French and Russo-Czech mutual aid treaties of 1935. But these had no substance in them—certainly nothing in the slightest degree comparable to Rapallo.

To cope with this situation three answers emerged—the first was Soviet isolationism backed by the call to revolution. The Soviet Union would rely on its own strength to confront a world in arms, call to its support the proletariat of the world, and watch with equanimity the internecine struggles of the capitalist powers.[60] Then there was co-operative action with the Western powers. Lastly, there was the effort to revert to some sort of Rapallo policy with Germany. It was quite clear to Coulondre, the French Ambassador in Moscow, that there were several Russian irons in the fire, several strings to the Russian bow.[61]

Each policy, of course, excluded the other two. But no stark choice presented itself—not even in 1939 and still less in earlier years. Until Munich, it seems, the emphasis was placed on collective security. But for Munich, Stalin told Byrnes at Yalta, there would have been no Russo-German pact.[62] But if, beyond all doubt, Munich marked a turning-point in Soviet disillusion with the West, it is also true that the beginnings of the quest for some sort of understanding with Germany do in fact antedate Munich. A thin red line can be traced back to 1935.

At this time it became clear to German diplomats in Moscow that Russian policy spoke with two discordant, contradictory voices. They issued respectively from Molotov and Litvinov.

The former's speeches, according to Schulenburg, showed that 'the Soviet Union was not desirous of breaking the bridge to an understanding with Germany'. Molotov's comments on Germany were 'couched in a more conciliatory tone than certain of Litvinov's declarations which were influenced by a strong personal resentment. . .'. Molotov gave the impression, Schulenburg continued, as though Russia 'wished to draw French attention to the fact that the relationship to Germany within the framework of Soviet foreign policy was not, for example, to be quite written off'.[63] At the end of 1935, Twardowski, the German counsellor of embassy, was more emphatic in noting that Litvinov's policy of encircling Germany was counteracted by 'other circles . . . which would like to find a *modus vivendi* with Germany because they hold the view that the breaking of all the bridges to Germany would be bound up with too great a danger for the Soviet Union'.[64]

Further evidence of these two trends came in both private and public Soviet declarations between 1935 and 1937. In the former year Kandelaki, the Soviet trade representative in Berlin, broke into a conversation with Schacht on financial matters to ask 'whether it was not possible also to improve the political relations between Germany and Russia'.[65] This was in July. In December it was the turn of Suritz, the Russian Ambassador in Berlin and of Bessonov, his counsellor of embassy, to tackle Twardowski on the same subject and to pose the same question: how could Russo-German political relations be improved? Bessonov thought this might result from Russia's forthcoming economic negotiations. Suritz asked whether Twardowski thought 'an elaboration of the Berlin Treaty possible, what effect a strengthening of economic relations would have on the political situation, whether a development of cultural relations was possible, whether he should intensify his social activity'.[66]

In December 1936 and again in January 1937 Kandelaki, in a conversation with Schacht made a further strong plea for a return to Russo-German harmony. 'The Russian government', he said, 'did not take up the standpoint of directing its policy against German interests. The Russian government was ready to enter into negotiations with the Reich government on the improvement of mutual relations and on general peace. Should the Reich government wish such negotiations to proceed by way of their respective diplomatic representatives, the Soviet government would raise no objections. The Russian government was ready at the wish of the German government to handle all discussions and negotiations confidentially and not publicly . . . Herr Kandelaki . . . asked me', Schacht's report continues, 'to ascertain however, whether there existed any prospect for the opening of talks in accordance with the existing Russian declarations. He would then immediately cause matters to proceed further' (*das Weitere veranlassen*).[67]

This dichotomy in Russian policy towards the Nazis, as between the hostility embodied in the theory of collective security and the attempt at a secret understanding was paralleled in public declarations. At the beginning of 1936, for example, Molotov made a most strange speech. He denounced, it is true, the foreign policy of *Mein Kampf*, its 'criminal propaganda for the seizure of foreign territory', the transformation of Germany into 'a military camp'. But he then struck a somewhat different tune. There was a 'contradictory situation' in present-day Germany. Molotov pointed out that on the German initiative a five-year credit of 200 million marks had been extended to the Soviet Union. Even larger credits were being discussed. 'The development of commercial and economic relations with other States,' Molotov commented, 'irrespective of the political forces that are temporarily ruling those countries, is in conformity with the policy of the Soviet Government. We think that it is also in keeping with the interests of the German people, and it is the business of the government of Germany, of course, to draw practical conclusions from this.' [68]

Later in 1936, on the morrow of the re-militarisation of the Rhineland, there came a further intimation of two contradictory Soviet policies. Litvinov denounced the German move in such uncompromising terms as to leave virtually no loophole for any accommodation with Nazi Germany. He denied that he was war-mongering. But he also said that peace in Europe would in no wise gain from the re-militarisation of the Rhineland, 'the less so if it is carried out unilaterally, in breach of obligations voluntarily undertaken by Germany. Neither the foreign policy of the present German Government nor the preaching of aggression and international hatred, and the glorification of the spirit of war, initiated and ceaselessly maintained in Germany during the last three years, permit us to make such an assertion.' Germany's aim, said Litvinov, was to establish 'the hegemony of Germany over the whole European continent. . .'.[69]

Contrast this with an interview given by Molotov a few days earlier. It is by no means Hyperion-Litvinov to satyr-Molotov, but it is markedly different in tone. There is no formal contradiction, but there is clearly a different emphasis. 'There is a tendency', Molotov told Chastenet of *Le Temps*, 'among certain sections of the Soviet public, towards an attitude of thoroughgoing irreconcilability to the present rulers of Germany, particularly because of the ever repeated hostile speeches of German leaders against the Soviet Union. But the chief tendency, and the one determining the Soviet Government's policy, thinks an improvement in Soviet-German relations possible.' As a means to this end, Molotov suggested that Germany might re-enter the League, provided real proof of a peaceful policy were forthcoming. 'Even Hitler's Germany?' asked Chastenet. 'Yes, even Hitler's Germany', replied Molotov.[70]

But these *ballons d'essai* never rose off the ground, these outstretched hands met with no answering German clasp. Neurath, the German Foreign Minister, wrote to Schacht that talks on the lines proposed by Kandelaki would be pointless and would enable Russia to attain a closer military alliance with France and possibly even 'a closer rapprochement with Britain. It would be different if affairs in Russia were to develop further in the direction of an absolute despotism, based on the military. In that case we must not miss the moment once again to insert our way into Russia' (*uns in Russland wieder einzuschalten*).[71]

In 1937 the Russian proposals were premature. There was as yet no need for the Germans to resume the old position so long as they could continue to count on Western acquiescence. The Russians therefore failed to win back Germany from the ranks of the West. Not until the end of 1938 did such a Russo-German rapprochement even begin to become a practical possibility. In the meantime, it may be presumed, these forces within the Soviet government which had all along preferred a German to a Western rapprochement were strengthened by the failure of

Litvinov's policy—a failure all the more hazardous because it left the Soviet Union exposed in the west at a time when it was also exposed to unremitting pressure in the east, from Japan. Events in the course of 1938 made this peril all the more real.

Early in that year, for example, on the morrow of the *Anschluss*, Litvinov's attempt to summon a conference of Russia, the United States, France, Great Britain and Czechoslovakia was frustrated by Chamberlain's rejection of the project. A conference of selected states would, he told the House of Commons, only increase international tension; and a conference of all European powers was impossible.[72] Chamberlain was reaffirming his quasi-unalterable rejection of all contact with the Soviets. 'His dislike of the Soviet Union was unmistakable', wrote Dirksen in June 1938; and three weeks later he again noted 'the desire on the part of the British Government . . . to exclude Soviet Russia from any discussion on a European settlement'.[73]

In March the Russian response to the rejection of Litvinov's suggestion of a European conference was already leading Davies to conceive of the 'far-fetched' possibility of a Russo-German alliance—'but it is quite within the range of the possibilities of the future'.[74] The Munich settlement brought this special aspect of the future perceptibly nearer and helped to disengage the Soviet Union from whatever attachment still bound it to the Western powers. This coincided with a major shift in German policy—away from seeking to achieve its aims in collaboration with the Western powers and towards the achievement of a similar relationship *vis-à-vis* Russia. In this evolution there are no dramatic turning-points—merely what Weizsäcker termed 'a slow and steady development'.[75] To add to the mystery, much of Soviet policy in the six months following Munich is more than usually opaque.

After Munich, as before, the Soviet Union, according to Schulenburg, continued to look on Germany as its 'chief opponent'. The Franco-Soviet pact had lost its value, following the French abandonment of Czechoslovakia. Czechoslovakia itself was looked on as 'a German satellite which is to serve as the springboard for the subsequent advance of Germany' and the Carpatho-Ukraine (the extreme eastern portion of Czechoslovakia) as 'a crystallizing point for a Ukrainian independence movement'. In this menacing situation, Schulenburg continued, the Soviets turned to Poland and reaffirmed the non-aggression pact of 1932. They thereby hoped 'to drive a wedge into German-Polish relations . . . to break Poland loose from the front of the aggressor states. . .'. In this way Russia would 'push back any future German offensive in the east from the Polish-Soviet to the German-Polish frontier'.[76] In conformity with this policy, the Russian aim continued to be to counteract the threat from its 'chief opponent' by attempted co-operation with the Western powers—the suggestion for a six-power conference after the occupation of Prague, for example, or the negotiations with Britain and France in the spring and summer of 1939.

But there was also the consideration that, left by the Western powers to face Germany alone, the Russians might, as Coulondre put it, 'détourner le Reich de l'Ukraine en le menant en Pologne. . .'.[77] The Russian rapprochement with Poland could not but strengthen any German policy conceived in these terms. It was, presumably, as clear to Hitler as it had been to Brüning and Stresemann, that the solution of the Corridor problem was 'hardly conceivable without the co-operation of Russia and Germany'.[78]

Be that as it may, of most importance in the perspective of late 1938 were suggestions, hints and feelers, growing in significance, that the best method of dealing with the German menace was by association with it—'bargaining with the aggressor', Stalin would later call it.[79] Side by side with Russia's pro-Polish orientation and the last attempts to form a common front with the Western powers, went the development of an attitude of aloof neutrality.[80] In February 1939 Litvinov was most explicit on this point to Sir William Seeds, the new British Ambassador in Moscow. 'Soviet government and people', he said, 'saw no sign whatever that France and Great Britain would do anything but capitulate; Soviet Union would therefore "keep aloof" all the more readily as their interests were not directly threatened.' [81]

Against this background what seems to have been the first positive step towards a Russo-German rapprochement was made. It took the form of an unofficial and informal agreement to cease mutual vilification of the respective heads of state in press and radio.[82] Another straw in the wind was the German proposal to transform the Anti-Comintern Pact into a general military alliance rather than leave it as an anti-Russian alliance *tout court*. Linked with this, and of the same tenor, was the German refusal to entertain a Hungarian request, made on the occasion of Hungary's adherence to the Pact, that the German Ambassador be withdrawn from the Soviet Union. 'Although the idea of a common gesture is worth considering,' wrote Weizsäcker, 'the proposed method did not seem practicable.' [83]

Nothing positive issued from these interchanges and intimations. Indeed, when Russia and Germany did agree to open trade negotiations at the end of December, they soon ran into difficulties, though of a technical nature, from the German side. The Germans decided that they be not 'completely broken off' but 'continued in a dilatory fashion'.[84] Enough remained, however, for Sir Alexander Cadogan—he wrote before the suspension of the trade talks—to point to the necessity of watching 'very carefully the development of any tendency towards a rapprochement between Germany and the Soviet'.[85]

This period of suspended animation would not last long. Within the next two months three separate events jerked it into motion—Stalin's speech of March 10th, 1939, Hitler's march into Prague on March 15th and the British guarantee to Poland on March 31st. Even when taken together these three factors by no means transformed the situation nor did they rid it of its fluidity—rather they gave fresh strength to certain phenomena, caused others to diminish in importance and thereby helped to shape the pattern of the future. Stalin's speech brought perceptibly nearer a rapprochement with Germany; the march into Prague contributed most powerfully to unmasking and discrediting Hitler; and the guarantee to Poland almost—but not quite—signified the abandonment of the British endeavour to achieve British aims in co-operation with Germany. The upshot was immediately clear, even before the implications had fully worked themselves out. It was on April 3rd that Hitler ordered the *Wehrmacht* to make itself ready for the attack on Poland.[86] A month later came the dismissal of Litvinov; and this inaugurated the first groping phase of serious Russo-German negotiations.

Stalin's speech recapitulated the themes dominating Russian

foreign policy over the last few years. It could be read in a number of different ways—as a reaffirmation of neutrality, of aloofness from the second imperialist war, as a manifesto of support for 'nations which are the victims of aggression and are fighting for the independence of their country', and as a gesture towards Germany. In foreign affairs he began by castigating the Western powers for their connivance in Fascist aggression, even their encouragement to aggression. They were, he said, 'egging the Germans on to attack further east, promising them easy pickings and prompting them: "just start a war against the Bolsheviks and everything will be all right" '. He then referred to 'the hullabaloo' in Britain, France and the United States over the Soviet Ukraine. It was said that the Germans, Stalin commented, 'now had what is called the Carpathian Ukraine, with a population of some seven hundred thousand, and that not later than this spring the Germans would annex the Soviet Ukraine. . . . It looks as if the object of this suspicious hullabaloo', Stalin continued, 'was to incense the Soviet Union against Germany, to poison the atmosphere and to provoke a conflict with Germany without any visible grounds.' Stalin, to conclude, emphasised the Russian desire to support the victims of aggression and to develop peaceful relations with all countries possessed of a similar desire.[87]

Anything or nothing could be made of this speech. To what use would it be put? There was soon little doubt on this point. Kirk, the United States chargé d'affaires in Moscow, said of Stalin's accusation that the Western powers were trying to embroil Russia in a war with Germany that it had 'given rise to the opinion that the Soviet Union . . . has publicly announced that if Germany refrains from a direct threat to the Soviet frontiers . . . . she may count on Soviet neutrality in the event of war against the Western powers'.[88] The German withdrawal was confirmed by developments in the Carpatho-Ukraine (Ruthenia).

Following Munich, German influence in this easternmost tip of Czechoslovakia had been used to organise the German minority and launch a Ukrainian nationalist movement. Yet when it came to the point, with the German annexation of the remainder of Czechoslovakia, Ruthenia was left to the Hungarians.

F

The Carpatho-Ukrainian government proclaimed its independence on March 15th and requested the protection of the Reich. To this appeal it received a dusty answer: 'As matters stand,' wired Weizsäcker the same afternoon, 'the German Government regrets that it is not in a position to assume the protectorate.' [89]

It is not as yet possible to determine how far German policy in Ruthenia was already conditioned by the hope or prospect of an alliance with Russia. Probably not very much, in such positive terms. But it *is* clear that such an alliance would never have come about had it not been for the German renunciation. Movement towards a decision could in no event be longer delayed.

The Russians were slowly moving away from a position of aloofness towards a certain identification with German aims. A second great swing in the interlocking structure of European power, comparable to that of 1929–33, was in motion. A minor diplomatic offensive in Berlin gave it added impetus. How senseless it was for ideological hair-splitting to lead to Russo-German conflict! How unimportant was ideology in Russian foreign policy! How necessary that Russo-German relations be normalised—these were the themes broached by a number of Russian diplomats in Berlin in April 1939.[90] They were taking up where Kandelaki and Suritz had left off. In early May, following the dismissal of Litvinov, the Russian Ambassador in Berlin tried to discover what effect, if any, this also might have on the German attitude to Russia.[91] Beneš, in May 1938, had warned the British Ambassador in Prague that 'an attempt to exclude Russia completely from Europe would be disastrous and would only force her to make an agreement with Germany against the rest of Europe'.[92] This was fast coming true. A Berlin Treaty would fast follow a Locarno Pact.

According to Hitler, the Russian change in personnel was 'decisive'.[93] The fact is that Hitler had created a situation whence the only issue was war. The Poles had rejected German demands for the cession of Danzig and for an extra-territorial roadway and railway across the Polish Corridor. The occupation of Prague had profoundly compromised the policy of appeasement to which Hitler had owed so much of his success. Then came the alignment of Poland with the Western powers; and on April

28th Hitler denounced the Anglo-German Naval Agreement and the German-Polish Pact of Non-Aggression.

No wonder, therefore, and all the more so in view of existing Soviet encouragement, that Hitler should turn to Russia as the solution to his difficulties. A mere two days after Litvinov's dismissal, he questioned Hilger, a member of the German Embassy in Moscow, as to the possibility of Stalin's readiness for an understanding with Germany.[94] But on May 20th, when Schulenburg, in accordance with special instructions from Ribbentrop and Hitler, attempted to resume the trade negotiations broken off in February, he was told by Molotov that 'the necessary political bases' must first be constructed.[95] For all that, Hitler was confident enough to anticipate a situation in which 'it was not out of the question that Russia might show itself disinterested in the destruction of Poland'.[96] This was on May 23rd. It needed three months, in fact, to reach this consummation—three months of confused and, at times, inconclusive negotiations. The Russians had been first to take the initiative. Later it fell to the Germans. But by comparison with the overwhelming significance of the Russo-German rapprochement in itself, it is unimportant and unnecessary to choose between the leader and the led. *Eo ipso*, the rapprochement signified the reversion to the pattern of the twenties: Germany could pursue its revisionist campaign unhampered by any eastern threat; in return Russia would be left in peace. This restored to the Russians their defensive German *point d'appui*.

V

Earlier in the year Chamberlain and Halifax had been able to contemplate with serenity a German invasion of the Ukraine; now Stalin, with equal serenity, could contemplate German hostilities against Britain and its allies. By virtue of Stalin's victory, the policy of appeasement had suffered overwhelming defeat.[97] The British guarantee to Poland, although something of the sort had been mooted during the previous fortnight, is best described as 'an improvisation'.[98]

In this somewhat casual way a revolution in British foreign policy was inaugurated. Not even in 1920 had any British

Foreign Secretary or Prime Minister committed his country, 'in the event of any action which clearly threatened Polish independence . . . at once to lend the Polish government all support in their power'. 'A revolutionary change', said Maisky[99]; 'a new epoch', said Chamberlain.[100] Indeed it was —such a commitment, at such a time.

But that it signified the end of the appeasement policy was not yet clear. The Russian government, in its dual and parallel negotiations with both the British and the Germans in the spring and summer of 1939, had to consider the advantages of the one as against the other.[101] This held good for Britain also. A similar dual policy developed. It was necessary to assess the value of an agreement *with* Germany as compared with that of an agreement *against* Germany. In the end, of course, the latter won. But not before Britain had made efforts to achieve the former.

There was a last British fling at appeasement by way of coming to an accommodation with Hitler. The then Sir Samuel Hoare (later Viscount Templewood), a member of the Inner Cabinet, defined British aims as a 'double policy of peace and rearmament. . . . In a sense the two aims were contradictory, often difficult and sometimes almost impossible to reconcile.'[102]

The most notable attempt to achieve this reconciliation—it was in fact a compromise that veered heavily in favour of appeasement—was made by Sir Horace Wilson in July 1939. 'In the present situation', he declared, 'it ought not to be a question of political manœuvres but of realising one of the greatest political combinations it was possible to imagine.'[103] This was no exaggeration. Could Britain, at this final hour, snatch back Germany? This was truly a grandiose vision, indeed one of the greatest of all political combinations. To bring it about, Wilson proposed, as pre-condition, a number of measures to restore confidence. On the negative side, this would include the abatement of German press attacks and speeches, and the relaxation of mobilisation. As a positive contribution, Wilson asked, could Hitler not 'give a lead to Europe designed to substitute harmony and security for the present state of friction and apprehension?' Hitler might, for example, Wilson suggested, 'set up some form of autonomy or home rule for Bohemia and Moravia'.[104] Given this presupposition, Wilson looked forward to 'an Anglo-German agreement involving renunciation of aggression *vis-à-vis* third powers [which] would completely absolve the British government from the commitments to which it was now pledged by the guarantee to Poland, Turkey, etc.; these commitments were assumed only against the event of attack, and were so formulated. With the removal of the danger the commitments would also cease to be operative.' [105]

In other words, as Dirksen put it, 'agreement with Germany would enable Britain to extricate herself from her predicament in regard to Poland on the ground that the non-aggression pact protected Poland from German attack; England would thus be relieved of her commitments. Then Poland, so to speak, would be left to face Germany alone.' [106]

To ask Hitler to make some gesture of confidence, however vacuous, in the summer of 1939, was a desperate fling. But, providing of course that he renounced aggression, he was certainly offered every inducement by the British. Such inducement included mutual declarations of non-interference in the British Empire and *Gross-Deutschland*, the latter requiring 'careful political wording' where east and south-east Europe were concerned; it included 'opening up the colonial question as a whole'; and air and army agreements which 'should take into account the special strategic and military conditions of the British Empire and of the Great German Reich in Central Europe'. The inducement 'would, above all, extend to the economic development of three great markets:

>The British Empire (especially India, South Africa, Canada, Australia).
>China (in co-operation with Japan).
>Russia (assuming that Stalin's policy develops accordingly)'. [107]

To shuffle off the guarantee to Poland and such peripheral matters as the Anglo-Russian negotiations, to proclaim British disinterest in Central and Eastern Europe and to propose Anglo-German economic development of Russia, 'providing Stalin's policy develops accordingly', was indeed the last and greatest fling in the appeasement policy.

It came too late. This last attempt to win back Germany to a policy of co-operation with Britain made no impact in Berlin. By now the die was cast for war—a war in which the struggle for Germany would move from the diplomatic to the military level and culminate in the physical partition of Germany. Germany involved both her suitors in a common struggle. Each emerged from the contest with half a loaf. The war was in this sense the conclusion or culmination of the First World War. Germany had then been saved by Russian weakness; but in the Second World War Russian strength made good the effects of that earlier collapse.

CHAPTER V

DIPLOMACY BECOMES WAR

FOR the period of the phoney war Soviet historians attribute to the British and French such aims as were considered consistent with pre-war western policies. To Ivanov, for example, 'even after the conclusion of the Soviet-German pact, Britain, France and the United States continued to bank on the possibility of a conflict between Germany and the U.S.S.R., after which they counted on elaborating a compromise anti-Soviet "peace"'.[1]

Other Soviet historians take a contrary view or one that would at least be difficult to reconcile with the first. It has been argued, for example, that the motive of Western publicists in elaborating plans in the earlier part of the war (1939–43) to dismember a defeated Germany was to crush 'an imperialist rival'. In the war's later phase, however, when Germany was losing, a softer mood prevailed, lest a possible future ally against Russia be unnecessarily and wilfully destroyed.[2]

It is certainly true that the theories and analyses of peace by no means disappeared with the advent of war; they were in fact translated into action at an accelerated pace. War telescoped development. The struggle for Germany—a topic of diplomacy for decades of peace—became a physical reality in but four years of war, taking shape as the partition of Germany. In 1941, as in 1914, it was well to the fore in Russian thinking.

Almost from the first, Stalin urged that 'the post-war organisation of peace . . . be founded' on the principle of preventing any recurrence of German aggression.[3] This formed part of a comprehensive outline by Stalin to Eden of the Soviet concept of the peace settlement. Stalin made this exposé at the end of 1941 in discussing an Anglo-Soviet treaty of alliance.

Other Soviet proposals included the recognition of the Russian incorporation of the Baltic States and Bessarabia, and the recognition of the Russo-Finnish frontier of 1941. The Curzon Line should form the Russo-Polish frontier; and from Rumania Stalin demanded special facilities for bases. In the case of Germany he proposed the restoration of Austria as an independent state, the detachment of the Rhineland from Prussia as an independent state or a protectorate, and possibly the constitution of an independent state of Bavaria. He also proposed the transfer of East Prussia to Poland and the return of the Sudetenland to Czechoslovakia. All this was accompanied by sundry other proposals regarding Greece, Turkey, Albania and Bulgaria. As a counterpart to the recognition of the Soviet Union's own special interests, Stalin 'was prepared to support any special arrangements for securing bases, etc., for the United Kingdom in Western European countries—e.g. France, Belgium, the Netherlands, Norway and Denmark'.[4]

It was optimistic to raise such issues at this time. Russia had its back to the wall, militarily speaking; also, Stalin's proposals met with the fiercest American opposition. The British, on the whole, after some hesitation, took up a more sympathetic attitude. They argued that post-war co-operation with Russia, as derived from the acceptance of Stalin's claims, was desirable to frustrate any Russo-German collaboration; it would 'recreate some reasonable balance of power in Europe, destroyed by the collapse of France, against the possibility of revived Germany'; and it would ensure the military encirclement of Germany. It was also thought advisable for Russia to be established on the Baltic 'to be able better to dispute with Germany the naval command of that sea. . .'.[5] Halifax, now the British Ambassador to Washington, saw Russia as a factor in the post-war balance of power against Germany.[6]

To the Americans the British attitude was 'not only indefensible from every moral standpoint but likewise extraordinarily stupid'. Sumner Welles expected the first acceptance of the Russian demands to be followed at once by further demands relating to Bukovina, Bessarabia, Eastern Poland and Northern Norway.[7] The fact is that Stalin's proposals to Eden raised a tremendous problem in the eyes of the American government: What were the limits of Soviet power? This was the reality behind the talk of the Atlantic Charter. 'If the British Government', ran a State Department memorandum of February 1942, 'with the tacit or expressed approval of this Government, should abandon the principle of no territorial commitments prior to the peace conference, it would be placed in a difficult position to resist additional Soviet demands relating to frontiers, territory, or to spheres of influence which would almost certainly follow wherever the Soviet Government would find itself in a favourable bargaining position. There is no doubt that the Soviet Government has tremendous ambitions with regard to Europe, and that at some time or other the United States and Great Britain will be forced to state that they cannot agree, at least in advance, to all its demands. It would seem that it is preferable to take a firm attitude now, rather than to retreat and to be compelled to take a firm attitude later when our position had been weakened by the abandonment of the general principle referred to above.' [8]

In practice, a 'firm attitude' signified present intransigence coupled with pie in the post-war sky. Russian security would be assured through 'a strong post-war peace organisation', and German disarmament.[9]

Pressure on Britain was unremittingly maintained by the Americans. The same pressure, in its turn, was transmitted to the Russians; and the Russians eventually gave way. The proposed Anglo-Russian treaty was whittled down from a territorial agreement into a twenty-year alliance. This does not seem, despite all Stalin's earlier efforts, to have disappointed the Russians unduly. Stalin, said Churchill, was 'almost purring'.[10] *Bolshevik* commented that the treaty 'considerably widens the scope of Anglo-Russian co-operation, extending it not only to military operations but also to the solution of post-war questions. The agreement looks forward to collaboration in the working out of the peace treaty and also to the achievement in the post-war world of the principles embodied in the Atlantic Charter.' [11]

This, it seems, puts a brave face on a Soviet diplomatic defeat. But the desire to secure recognition of the incorporation of the Baltic States was by no means abandoned, only postponed.[12] Thus the Western, primarily American, policy of temporising, of putting the *status quo* on ice, as it were, proved increasingly untenable. It would not be possible to postpone to a remote peace settlement all the territorial and other problems that arose in the course of the war. More and more, the very discussion of these problems came to reflect and express the divergent policies of the Allies. The pattern of 1941/42 would recur: on the one side an attempt at postponement, on the other an attempt to fix the shape of the future in definite commitments.

Germany, of course, eventually took a central place in these allied interchanges. But in 1942 and for part of 1943, this was by no means so evident; naturally enough. Until the battle of Stalingrad had been won, post-war planning for Germany was wholly academic. 'First catch your bear, then skin it' runs the Russian proverb.

However, even when the bear was only half-caught, its skinning became a recurrent topic at high-level allied conferences. The idea of partitioning Germany, originally launched by Stalin at the end of 1941, showed itself a hardy growth. The idea was not everywhere welcome, of course. There was fluctuation and fluidity on all sides, until the very end of the war. This testified to the inherent ambivalence of partition, to the ambiguity it embodied and to the manner in which its realisation might or might not fit into opposing conceptions of the post-war European order.[13]

In 1941–42 the tussle over the Anglo-Russian treaty of alliance had already disclosed a conflict over the limits of Soviet power. It had primarily had reference to Russia's Baltic conquests. Now it developed implications that would slowly begin to draw Germany within its orbit, or at least raise the question of Germany as a factor in some sort of European balance. In 1943, two conceptions prevailed of the policy that would best preserve peace in post-war Europe—the policy of a balance in Europe and the policy of dismembering Germany. In the early part of the war, when Germany seemed all-powerful and Russia the weaker party, Halifax had sought to strengthen Russia against Germany.[14] Now, just as consistently, following the battle of Stalingrad, British policy sought to achieve a balance against Russia. 'It was important', Churchill told a gathering of United States political leaders, 'to re-create a strong France; for the prospect of having no strong country on the map between England and Russia was not attractive'. In the same strain he spoke of the need for Great Britain and the U.S. 'to be associated in some way in the policing of Europe'; he spoke of the need for a Danubian Federation to be based on Vienna, to compensate for the disappearance of the Austro-Hungarian Empire and to include perhaps Bavaria; he proposed, too, a Balkan Federation, the separation of Prussia from Germany and a Poland and Czechoslovakia 'standing together in friendly relations with Russia'.[15]

Churchill combines his preference for larger political units with a modified form of dismemberment. Elsewhere the emphasis is reversed. In March 1943, for example, during a visit to Washington, Eden found Roosevelt in favour of dismemberment as a solution to the German problem. Eden also noted that this policy coincided with that of Stalin—a fact confirmed by Maisky and Litvinov.[16]

But on the Western side at least, all remained informal and inconclusive. When Eden next discussed the German future, at the first Quebec Conference in August 1943, he himself was considerably less enthusiastic. The majority of the British Cabinet also opposed dismemberment on the grounds of impracticability. But, if voluntary, then it was desirable. Hull, for the Americans, agreed with this, citing in his support the recommendation of a State Department advisory committee. This report also left room for a certain measure of decentralisation in so far as southern Germany, it was hoped, might be prized loose from the north by giving it a Mediterranean outlet such as Fiume or Trieste. Eden, for his part, echoed Churchill in advocating the restoration in some form of the Austro-Hungarian Empire as 'a Danubian group'.[17]

This plan was conceived without the support of Roosevelt or Sumner Welles, both of whom were outspoken advocates of dismemberment. The President favoured a division of Germany into three or more sovereign states joined by various economic arrangements but deprived of all armament industries and military training.[18] (But Roosevelt also stated that there was bound to be a period of trial and error and that partition might have to be abandoned.) The Welles plan provided for partition into a south-west state, a north-west state and a north-east state. East Prussia would fall to Poland.[19]

At Teheran, there was yet another repetition of the well-worn standpoints. Churchill was 'all for' dismemberment. But he was 'primarily interested', he said, 'in seeing Prussia, the evil core of German militarism, separated from the rest of Germany'. The first was a destructive consideration, the second constructive in that Churchill hoped 'to detach Bavaria, Baden and Württemberg and the Palatinate from the rest of Germany and make them part of the confederation of the Danube'.

Roosevelt spoke of splitting Germany into five self-governing parts—Prussia, which was 'to be rendered as small and as weak as possible'; Hanover and North-west Germany; Saxony and the Leipzig area; Hesse-Darmstadt, Hesse-Cassel and the section south of the Rhine; Bavaria, Baden and Württemberg. In addition, the Kiel Canal and Hamburg, and the Ruhr and the Saar would come under the control of the United Nations or some form of international control.

Stalin gave no comparable outline. But he indicated strongly that, while preferring Roosevelt's, he thought both suggestions inadequate, that neither would destroy the German urge to re-unite—'if Germany was to be dismembered it should really be dismembered'. He took particular exception to Churchill's proposal to include parts of Germany in a confederation, for this 'would merely offer an opportunity to the German elements to revive a great State . . . to create large frameworks within which the Germans could operate would be very dangerous'. Altogether, Stalin opposed in principle the idea of confederation as 'artificial and one that would not last in that area. . . .' He took on the surprising rôle of the defender of the right of small nations to autonomy: 'Austria, for example, had existed as an independent state and should again. Hungary, Rumania and Bulgaria likewise. . . .'

Did Stalin then contemplate 'a Europe composed of little states, disjointed, separated and weak?' asked Churchill. 'Not Europe but Germany', replied Stalin. Roosevelt remarked that 'Germany had been less dangerous to civilisation when in 107 provinces'. But Churchill stuck to his preference for 'larger units'.[20]

Of more significance here than the actual discussion of Germany is the framework of larger units as against small, in which it had its setting. This brush had occurred before. Earlier in 1943 Maisky had made precisely the same point to Eden [21]; and at Moscow, Molotov had drawn a not altogether unjustifiable comparison between 'some of the plans for federations' and the old *cordon sanitaire* policy.[22]

No sooner did this view gain currency than a counter-campaign was launched in the Soviet press. Manuilsky, for example, taking the Russo-Czech treaty, which had been recently signed, as the model for relations between Russia and other states, praised it for delivering 'a heavy blow' to plans for an East European federation—a federation which would, he said, 'create new sources of war in the centre of Europe'.[23] In other journals, regional groupings as part of a proposed East European federation—e.g. Czech-Polish or Greek-Yugoslav—were denounced as instruments of Polish reaction seeking 'to acquire a new fulcrum for the realisation of its projects'.[24] More explicitly, a warning was issued against the idea of a European balance of power, as propagated by certain 'reactionary circles' in Britain. It would lead to a 'compromise with the German bandits and the breakdown of collaboration between the Allies'.[25] In sum, those who promoted the federation of the smaller European states, were making common cause with reactionaries, Munichites and isolationists.[26]

What would this Russian policy mean? No better evaluation exists than that made by a member of the American Embassy in Moscow; 'Germany is to be broken up and kept broken up. The states of Eastern, South-Eastern and Central Europe will not be permitted to group themselves into any federations. France is to be stripped of her colonies and strategic bases beyond her borders and will not be permitted to maintain any appreciable military establishment. Poland and Italy will remain approximately their present territorial size, but it is doubtful if either will be permitted to maintain any appreciable armed force. *The result would be that the Soviet Union would be the only important military and political force on the Continent of Europe. The rest of Europe would be reduced to military and political impotence.*' [27]

II

The upshot of this discussion at Teheran remained inconclusive. Of greater relevance to the future was a United States memorandum produced at the previous Moscow Conference of Foreign Ministers. This was not intended to provide more than a basis for discussing the future of Germany, but it proved to have considerable long-term significance. It was here that the proposal was first made for the joint occupation and control of Germany, for the creation of an Inter-Allied Control Commission, the destruction of the Nazi Party, the destruction of any German war-making capacity, the payment of reparations and the installation of a democratic polity to safeguard the civil and political liberties of the individual.[28]

This scheme was not explicitly adopted but remitted to a new Inter-Allied body—the European Advisory Commission—with its seat in London. What now became of the utmost significance was the proclaimed intention of a joint occupation of Germany: for the elaboration in the European Advisory Commission of the zonal system of occupation set the pattern for the eventual partition.

Roosevelt commented at Yalta: '. . . The permanent treatment of Germany might grow out of the question of the zones of occupation, although the two were not directly connected.'[29] But a direct connection did establish itself. Zones and partition did become connected, through the lack of any policy for Germany as a whole, reinforced by the jockeying for position in Germany that characterised the closing stages of the war. This applied equally to the Anglo-American, the Russian, and the German armies. The zonal system, which was initially intended to be of limited duration, became perpetuated because Germany, once again the greatest stake in the struggle for European power, as earlier in 1919, was caught up in that struggle. In this ultimate phase, a certain contribution to the dismemberment of Germany was made by German military strategy itself. The unity that had been secured through blood and iron would be broken through blood and iron.

How did all this come about ? Before the eventual occupation system, with exclusively national contingents, was adopted, the

British made two proposals for the mixing-in of contingents from each of the Allied forces so that in each zone each ally would have been represented. A Foreign Office official made the first such proposal in Washington in December 1943. It was rejected, largely on technical gounds, at the behest of United States military opinion.[30] Sir William (now Lord) Strang made the second such proposal in the summer of 1944. This too the Americans opposed.[31]

The alternative was exclusively national zones, such as would later shape the pattern of the occupation.[32] The delimitation of the zones themselves was first discussed at the Cairo Conference that immediately followed Teheran.[33] But no sort of detail was elaborated until the European Advisory Commission met a month or so later. It was then that Strang, the British member of the Commission, proposed a Russian zone of occupation consisting of Mecklenburg-Pomerania, Brandenburg, Saxony-Anhalt, Thuringia, and areas to the east; a British zone to include Brunswick, Hesse-Nassau, the Rhine provinces and the areas northwards; and an American zone including the Saar and the Bavarian Palatinate west of the Rhine, together with Hesse-Darmstadt, Württemberg, Baden and Bavaria.[34] The area of Greater Berlin would come under joint occupation.

The Russians accepted this proposal the following month, in February 1944.[35] But they disputed with the British for two months over the fate of the Baltic island of Fehrmahn. In the end they had to acknowledge that it belonged with the province of Schleswig-Holstein to the British zone.[36] This conflict over a tiny Baltic island anticipated a more intensive conflict later.[37] But the major acceptance was seen by the West as a token of Russian moderation—all the more so as at this time the American War Department expected the war to end with the Soviets occupying all Germany up to the Rhine.[38]

Once the zones had been allocated between the Russians and the Western powers—though not as between the United States and Britain, a matter which would cause prolonged dispute—the next step was to define the occupation system and the machinery of control. This was achieved by mid-November, 1944.[39] No special friction showed itself. But there was some significant difference of opinion on the rôle of the Commander-in-

Chief. To the Soviets he was primarily the military governor of his zone and only secondarily a member of the supreme tripartite organ of control, the Control Council in Berlin. This conflicted with the Anglo-American view: '. . . We thought', writes Strang, 'that Germany ought, as far as possible, to be treated as a whole and that the separation of the zones ought not to be over-emphasised'.[40]

But if, by the end of 1944, there existed a scheme of zones— again disregarding the allocation of the two Western zones— and a scheme of occupation, there still existed no policy for Germany as a whole. In Winant's words to Roosevelt: 'It simply established the mechanics essential to any program that may be determined by those responsible for policy'.[41]

Pour comble de malheur, the President had himself, in the aftermath of the Morgenthau fiasco, foresworn any intention of 'making detailed agreements for a country which we do not yet occupy'.[42] In a similar vein, Roosevelt had also more or less surrendered hope of influencing conditions in the Russian-occupied sector of Germany 'unless there is some chance of some of the protests being heeded'.[43] Into this vacuum and this renunciation there flowed irresistibly, like a force of nature, the national policies of the occupying powers, turning each zone into a simulacrum of the occupier. If the Americans followed a policy of postponement, lest they be forced to recognise Russian *faits accomplis*, then postponement itself facilitated the creation of such *faits accomplis*. It was understandable therefore that Stalin should show no eagerness for a three-power conference in the summer of 1944;[44] or that Gusev, the Russian representative on the European Advisory Commission, should procrastinate for nine weeks at the beginning of 1945.[45] The tide was running fast in the Russian favour.

None the less, before national interests became the sole and unconcealed criterion almost a year had still to elapse. Further discussions and further plans for dismemberment filled this interval. When Churchill was at Moscow in October 1944 he found Stalin adumbrating a refined version of some earlier proposals. The Ruhr and Saar should be detached, said Stalin, 'put out of action', probably under international control and a separate state formed in the Rhineland. Stalin also proposed a federation of south German states, including Austria, Bavaria, Württemberg and Baden, with Vienna as their capital. Furthermore, Poland, Czechoslovakia, and Hungary would form a realm of independent, anti-Nazi, pro-Russian states. There was much here to appeal to Churchill, given his previous advocacy of a Danubian Federation.[46] But Stalin's *volte-face* in this matter perhaps owes more to the advance of the Soviet troops into the Balkans, whereby it might reasonably be anticipated that such a federation would come under Soviet influence.

Be that as it may, these were, in any event, only informal talks, of no binding nature. At the Yalta Conference a more formal arrangement was arrived at. And what was this more formal arrangement? A committee! 'The study of the question of the procedure of the dismemberment of Germany was referred to a committee consisting of Mr. Eden, Mr. Winant and F. T. Gusev.'[47] This was *not*, be it noted, a committee established to study dismemberment *tel quel*. What it had to do, in Churchill's words, was to proceed 'to a most rapid examination of the question of the best means of *studying* a *method* of dismemberment'.[48]

By now the idea of partitioning Germany was well-nigh stone dead. It received its *coup de grâce* when even Stalin declared in his *Proclamation to the Peoples* of May 9th, 1945: 'The Soviet Union celebrates victory but it does not intend to dismember or destroy Germany'.[49] At the Potsdam Conference the subject received not the slightest mention. 'By now', writes Byrnes, 'the thinking of all three governments had veered away from dismemberment.'[50] Truman's aim, in fact, had long been a Germany 'under one government'.[51] And what was on Stalin's agenda? With the very significant exception of reparations, such odds and ends as the Franco régime, Tangier, trusteeships for Russia, Syria and Lebanon, etc.[52]

What was the reason for Stalin's *volte-face*? Here, in the present state of the evidence, we can only conjecture. Stalin explained to Hopkins in May 1945 that he had foresworn partition because of British and American reluctance.[53] It would be so uncharacteristic of Stalin to abandon a policy in deference to opposition from his allies that we are justified in seeking another explanation. We probably find this in the problem of the future

G

status of the Ruhr. This undoubtedly constituted one of the most important aspects of the struggle for Germany. In Russian eyes it had over-riding importance as the source of the bulk of the reparations that Stalin intended to claim from Germany. Thus what Stalin required was either genuine three-power control of Germany or else some form of international statute for the administration of the Ruhr such as Stalin had himself proposed to Churchill in Moscow, or as Molotov put forward at Potsdam.[54] But if the zonal boundaries were to harden into *de facto* partition, as Roosevelt had already anticipated, then the Russians might find themselves excluded from any voice in the production of this part of the British zone. Thus, in a curious sort of way, the two sides changed shoes. The Americans replied to Stalin's demand for some say in the control of the Ruhr with a dusty answer. 'Under present circumstances', argued a State Department Briefing Book Paper, 'an extension of Soviet power and influence into the heart of Western Europe through the device of trusteeship would manifestly be open to grave doubt.'[55] When the matter was discussed during the actual conference, both Truman and Bevin opposed any special mention of the Ruhr and agreed that it would be administered under the Control Council—i.e., that it would in fact remain in the British zone subject to British authority.[56]

But whether or not Stalin's renunciation of dismemberment was the consequence of the Russian desire to acquire a foothold in the Ruhr, a dismembered Germany was fast becoming a reality on the battlefields. It was a world away from the 'mirage' that it has been claimed to be.[57] There was a process in motion that would represent the gigantic culmination of a struggle that had been in train since 1918. The contest for Germany that had passed through so many phases would at last reach its climax in the physical partition of the country.

III

How did the last phase come about? It has already been shown how the various Allied plans for Germany tentatively and gropingly reflected and incorporated the national interests of the particular power. To put it crudely, if Churchill favoured the

maintenance of German territorial integrity as a barrier to
Russian advance, in pursuit of the traditional British policy of
balance, it was likewise in Stalin's interest to favour a weak
or disunited Germany. But we need to delve more widely and
consider other areas of conflict opening up between the West
and Russia.

'Broadly speaking', Churchill wrote to Eden in May 1944,
'the issue is: are we going to acquiesce in the communisation of
the Balkans and perhaps of Italy?'[58] To this the reply came fast
—an unavoidable but undeniable 'yes'. Soon after D-Day in the
West, a Red Army offensive took Russian forces into Rumania,
Hungary, the Baltic States and Poland. Moreover, from the
Russian refusal, either to give direct aid to the Warsaw revolt or
to permit Anglo-American air aid, it could be deduced that the
Russians had no wish to find themselves confronted by a *fait
accompli* in Poland brought about by rival political forces. In
the Balkans, Churchill, with reluctant American acquiescence,
tried to save a remnant of Western influence through a bilateral
agreement with the Soviets. In May and October 1944, he negotiated with Stalin an agreement that would provide for Russian
predominance in Rumania and Bulgaria, British in Greece and
a fifty-fifty split in Hungary and Yugoslavia. This was intended
to be a 'temporary guide' to suit wartime conditions.[59]

This arrangement worked not inharmoniously in so far as it
enabled the British to crush, without Soviet intervention or protest, the Greek Communist revolt at the end of 1944. But a
similar tolerance was not extended to Russian action in Rumania,
where a Communist government was imposed in February 1945.
It was also noted, at the end of 1944, that 'the arrival of the Red
Army had drawn the Communist Tito back into the Russian
orbit . . .'[60]

What applied to the Balkans could also not but apply—and
all the more strongly—to Germany. Not only was Germany in-
comparably more important strategically and industrially; here
the Western Allies had troops on the ground, the absence of
which was a serious handicap elsewhere.

In the intervening period, before the Western armies were actually on German soil, the only substitute for troops, fragile though
it might appear, would be the boundaries of the occupation

zones. But by January 1945 no inter-governmental agreement
had yet been concluded. Winant feared, in the absence of such
an agreement, that 'the Russians might reach the border of
their zone and then keep on going'. Harry Hopkins and Stettinius, the new United States Secretary of State, agreed that this
was a matter of the 'utmost urgency'.[61] At the Anglo-American
Malta Conference, just before Yalta, the agreement was finally
signed. It came into force on February 6th, 1945.

As events turned out, it had no practical significance at all.
The boot was very much on the other foot. The Russian advance
into Germany soon encountered much stiffer resistance than
the Anglo-American. But this interchange is certainly significant
as the first intimation that the occupation zones might also be
barriers over contested territory.

The same indication of a struggle for Germany, but in far
stronger terms, is manifest in Stalin's accusation that the pre-
liminaries to the German surrender in Italy were in fact a preparation for an Anglo-American armistice which would release
German troops for reinforcements on the Eastern front.[62] There
was not the slightest ground for this accusation. But it would
have been nourished by the Anglo-American decision not to
admit Soviet officers to the preliminary negotiations 'for fear
that their presence would compromise the project'.[63]

In the end the capitulation was termed 'a tactical surrender'.
This was 'a device adopted to avoid the Soviet insistence that
we could not accept any surrender without all three powers participating in the negotiations'.[64]

During these negotiations Churchill had expressed understanding of a Russian fear lest the Anglo-American armies 'advance against little or no opposition, and will reach the Elbe, or
even Berlin before the Bear'. From this he concluded that, were
negotiations to break out on this, the main front, 'the Russians
should be in from the start . . .'.[65] But this did not preclude
the attempt to secure for the West the maximum political and
strategic advantage in defeated Germany. Churchill identified
this with the capture of Berlin by the Anglo-American forces
and their advance as far eastwards as possible: '. . . From a
political standpoint we should march as far east into Germany
as possible, and that should Berlin be in our grasp we should

certainly take it'.[66] This applied also to the capture of Prague 'and as much as possible of the territory of Western Czechoslovakia'. This, Churchill thought, 'might make the whole difference to the post-war situation in Czechoslovakia, and might well influence that in nearby countries'.[67] The climax came with the argument that, pending agreement on outstanding issues with the Russians, the Anglo-American armies should not withdraw from any position they occupied inside the Russian zone of occupation.[68] This had as implication Churchill's earlier remark: 'I hardly like to consider dismembering Germany until my doubts about Russia's intentions have been cleared away'.[69]

In the end, however, once the Rhine was crossed, Berlin was relegated to a secondary objective and the alternative strategy of a drive to Leipzig was adopted. The only concession to political considerations came with the advance on Lübeck. Spurred on by Churchill and Eisenhower, Montgomery's forces drove north-eastwards after the Rhine crossing. They reached the Baltic at Lübeck and Wismar on May 2nd, sealing off the Danish peninsula and the entrance to the Baltic from those Russian forces advancing hot-speed westwards from Stettin. There were only about six hours to spare.[70] In Czechoslovakia, Eisenhower, in deference to Soviet objections, refrained from liberating Prague and held the American forces to a line Karlsbad-Pilsen-Budejovice.[71]

At this stage of the occupation of Germany a certain part was taken by the Germans themselves. If political considerations helped, notably in the case of Lübeck and Stuttgart, to determine the advance of the West, it is reasonable to suppose that similar considerations prevailed on the Soviet side. (Certainly, their hostile attitude to Eisenhower's proposal to advance further eastwards into Czechoslovakia gives ground to this supposition.) But it was precisely in this that the Russians were frustrated. In the last stages of the war they had to face far stiffer resistance than the Western forces. It did not escape Stalin's notice that the Germans fought fanatically for 'an insignificant railway station' in Czechoslovakia but in the West they would, without resistance, yield up towns such as Mannheim, Cassel and Osnabrück.[72]

This military policy had its *raison d'être* in the German attempt to arrange a separate peace or armistice in the West and then, freed from the Anglo-American incubus, to continue the war against the Russians. This plan had first emerged in the foreign policy of the German resistance, or at least part of it.[73] Their successors in this endeavour were Goering, who planned to fly to Eisenhower on April 24th, 1945, with a plan for peace in the West;[74] and Himmler, who had a similar plan for peace with the West and war in the east.[75] Grand-Admiral Dönitz was the last and also the most consistent of the line. He took the policy of the German resistance to its logical conclusion. He began his short career as successor to Hitler by declaring that it was his 'first task to save the Germans from destruction by the advancing Bolshevik enemy. Only with this object does the military struggle continue. In so far and so long as the attainment of this objective is hampered by the British and Americans, we will defend ourselves against them also and continue the struggle. The Anglo-Americans are then not continuing the war for the sake of their own people, but solely to spread Bolshevism in Europe.'[76]

Dönitz himself had earlier moved naval forces from the North Sea and Norway to the Baltic. Here they could help to protect refugee transports from the eastern front.[77] A similar disposition had been made in the military field when the German Twelfth Army was withdrawn from the American front and moved eastwards just before the Soviets had completed the encirclement of Berlin. This disposition was not only military, but also political, writes one Soviet source, showing the Americans that 'all the remaining forces of Germany are being directed against the Soviet Union'.[78]

Consistent with this policy, it was Dönitz' aim 'to delay as long as possible a total capitulation which would have delivered the German armies on the eastern front into Russian captivity'.[79] He hoped to win an interval of 8–10 days before being forced to capitulate to the Russians; and to use this interval to arrange partial capitulations—'by no means in public' (*keinesfalls öffentlich*)—lest the Russians interfere.[80] This policy at first met with some success in that Montgomery accepted a German surrender covering all the German armed forces in Holland, North-west

Germany, including the Frisian Islands and Heligoland, and Denmark.

Dönitz, writes his adjutant, was 'encouraged' by this success and tried the same approach to Eisenhower.[81] But here Dönitz' emissaries met with a rebuff. Eisenhower would accept no surrender 'that did not involve simultaneous capitulation everywhere'.[82] All the Germans could achieve, alleging 'poor communications', was a delay of some 45 hours before total, unconditional surrender became effective on *all* fronts.[83] The instrument of surrender was signed on May 7th at 2.41 a.m., but it did not enter into force until 00.00 hours on May 9th.

Dönitz used this interval to order all German Army groups in the Central, South-east and Southern sectors to take no notice of the surrender in the West—'because the fight with the Western powers had lost its meaning, the only aim for which we must still fight is the salvation of as many Germans as possible from Bolshevisation and enslavement. That is your sacred task which you must and will fulfil in the sense of our dead Führer . . .'; and on May 8th he eventually ordered these groups to withdraw to the West, fighting their way, if necessary, through the Soviet lines and to surrender to the Anglo-American forces.[84] On that same day a second surrender ceremony took place before Marshal Zhukov in Berlin. But to the last the Germans maintained the distinction between the Western and Eastern fronts: the Berlin surrender was considered to have only 'a demonstrative and propagandist value'.[85]

The harshest Russian critics of Western policy concede, though not always graciously, that there was no semblance of a separate peace between Germany and the Western powers.[86] But the latter could clearly not prevent the Germans from fighting far more energetically on the Eastern than on the Western front. It is this aspect of German 'co-operation' with the Western Allies that gives some semblance of retrospective justification to the fears that Stalin had expressed at the time of the Italian negotiations.[87] Such 'co-operation' could not but spur him on to yet greater efforts to seize his own 'Lübecks', his own 'Stuttgarts'.[88] At Yalta, early in February 1945, he had told Churchill that the Red Army was already able to cross the Oder River. But this was not achieved until the middle of April.[89] In the interval Stalin was compelled to witness the contrast between his own fanatically contested advance and the relatively easy advance of the Western powers.

By facilitating or at least not offering stern resistance to the Western advance, and by combining this with a last-ditch defence against the Russians, the Germans created the maximum distrust between the Allies and ensured the maximum Russian pressure to hold their ground in Germany. In this way, the German attempt to split the Allies made its own distinctive and invaluable contribution to the partition of Germany. This was the solution that automatically resulted from the failure of either of the allied groupings to achieve the totality of its aims in Germany. If neither the Russians nor the Western powers could conquer the whole of Germany or at least secure a dominating position in the country, then partition was the only peaceful solution.[90] This was the end of a path which both Russia and the Western powers had first begun to tread more than thirty years earlier.

NOTE TO CHAPTER V

Did Stalin plan a separate peace of his own in 1943 ? In the first half of September 1943 the organ of the Free Germany Committee was authorised to publish an article entitled 'Armistice— the Need of the Hour'. This was 'virtually an offer of an armistice, however indirectly made, to the official authorities of Hitler's government'.[91] This move was accompanied, in the hidden background, by desultory Russo-German peace talks in Stockholm extending over almost a year—from the end of 1942 to the autumn of 1943. The supposed basis of an agreement would be a reversion to the Russo-German frontier of 1939 or 1914, a free hand in the Straits, German disinterest *vis-à-vis* Russian aspirations in Asia and extended Russo-German economic relations.[92]

To this threat came a sort of confirmation in the concluding phrase of Stalin's Order of the Day for January 25th, 1943, i.e. after the first contact with the German negotiator in Stockholm had already been made: 'Forward to the rout of the German invaders and their expulsion from the boundaries of our Mother-land', was his cry.[93]

But the Russian troops did cross the Russian frontiers; the talks in Stockholm came to naught; and the 'Armistice' article was never published. What, then, do we conclude from these episodes ? In all probability that they were intended to put pres-sure on the Western powers. This was one hypothesis advanced by Schulenburg to explain the negotiations in Stockholm; [94] and Eden thought Stalin's ambiguous Order of the Day was issued with an eye to the German home front.[95] But to certain Western minds the hypothesis of a separate Russo-German peace in 1942–43 remained plausible.[96] What, ultimately, seems to rule this out of court was Stalin's fear of Germany. His words to Mikolajczyk are illuminating. This was in August 1944: 'The Germans will rise again. They are a strong nation. From Bis-marck's triumph in 1871 they needed forty years to undertake new aggression. After its failure twenty or twenty-two years of regeneration were sufficient to repeat that once more—this time almost successfully. Now, who knows if after twenty or twenty-five years they will not be once more ready to fight. Yes, Ger-many is a strong country even though Hitler is weakening it. But the German economic and military staff will survive Hitler. It is our conviction that the danger from Germany may repeat itself. For this reason the present discussions which are going on in Washington about collective security are so urgent. I am for all possible and impossible repression of Germany. But in spite of this they may rise again. Therefore, one had to keep the sword ready. This sword will be a treaty between us and the forces provided by collective security.' [97]

NOTES AND REFERENCES

INTRODUCTION
[1] Ritter, 373

I—PROLOGUE IN PETROGRAD

[1] Mezhdunarodniye Otnosheniya, Series III, Vol. VI, Pt. I, No. 256, 247.
[2] *Ibid.* Pt. 2, No. 546, 111-12.
[3] Lloyd George, I, 948.
[4] Ribot, 93.
[5] Pingaud, III, 296.
[6] Im Dunkel, ed. Stieve, II, 260-2; Paléologue, III, 192-3; Pingaud, III, 302.
[7] Mezhdunarodniye Otnosheniya, Series III, Vol. VI, Pt. I, No. 526, 328.
[8] Lloyd George, I, 949.
[9] Parliamentary Debates, House of Commons, Fifth Series, Vol. 100, col. 2017 (December 19th, 1917).

II—THE RUSSIAN STAKE IN GERMANY

[1] Documents, ed. Degras, I, 7.
[2] House Papers, III, 161.
[3] Stuart, 80.
[4] Newton, 467-8. The relationship between Lansdowne's appeal and social conditions in 1917 is well brought out by Lloyd George. 'Lord Lansdowne', he writes, ' . . . represented a powerful and growing section of the people not only in social, but also in industrial circles. The suffering was not confined to one class. All classes alike shared the tortures of sorrow for the fallen, and the anxieties of incessant apprehension for those who were in the zone of death. Amongst the workmen there was an unrest that was disturbing and might at any moment become dangerous. The efforts we were making to comb out more men for the army were meeting with resistance among the Trade Unions, whose loyalty and patriotism had throughout been above reproach.' (Lloyd George, II, 1491.) This mood also made it necessary for Lloyd George to organise his conference on peace terms with the trade unions on January 5th, 1918. Trotsky had been publishing the secret treaties of the Allies and it was essential for Lloyd George to spike the Bolsheviks' guns and to 'prove' to the workers that they were not being 'combed out' to fight for the imperialist aims revealed by Trotsky. Hence also a conspiracy of silence about these treaties: Balfour, when pressed in the House of Commons, declared that 'the documents in question ought not to have been published and I do not propose to republish them' (Parliamentary Debates, House of Commons, Fifth

Series, Vol. 100, col. 1153 [December 12th, 1917]). *The Times* decided 'not to inconvenience the British, French and Italian Governments, and to maintain silence about the Secret Treaties; also as far as possible, to curtail its Petrograd correspondent's dispatches on the subject'. (*History of The Times*, IV, Part I, 344.)

5 Webb, 96-7. But at the very end of the war Webb also asked: 'are we confronted with another Russia in Austria, possibly even in Germany—a Continent in rampant revolution, over which there will be no Government to which we can dictate our terms?' (*ibid.* 133). Milner's views on the unlikelihood of complete military victory and the bases of a possible negotiated peace are described in Chapman-Huston, 268-70, 278-9.

6 *The Scotsman*, May 18th, 1918. It also seems that Smuts anticipated the situation at the end of the Second World War as furthered by the policy of unconditional surrender. From 1917 onwards he argued in favour of limited objectives in war on the grounds of maintaining stability in continental Europe. This meant restraint on the claims of France and of the latter's eastern clients and on the expansionism of Bolshevism. It also meant the maintenance of Germany as a strong state within the Allied orbit. Smuts also hoped to see the unity of the Danubian area retained (Hancock, 46-7). However purblind it was for Smuts to talk of stability at a time of unprecedented carnage, this is an example of his unacknowledged prescience. Critics of unconditional surrender make precisely the same point that Smuts made in 1917-18. His successors perceive, as one of them has written, that the principle of unconditional surrender 'ensured that the war against Germany would continue beyond the stage of military decision to the point of political collapse, and would not end until the Russian and Anglo-American armies met in the heart of the Continent' (Wilmot, 713).

7 Lloyd George, II, 1478 ff.

8 Trotsky, 3.

9 Chicherin (1), 5-6.

10 Documents Réunis, 160-1. There was, of course, nothing in the nature of a concerted capitalist attack on the Soviet Union. Mixed motives prevailed not only inside the Entente countries but also amongst them; and these distinctions could be exploited by the embattled Bolsheviks.

11 Radek, 'Noyabr', *Krasnaya Nov*, No. 10 (October 1926), 143-4.

12 Lenin, XXVIII, 83.

13 *Ibid.* 101 ff.

14 Chicherin (2), 23.

15 *Pravda*, October 27th, 1918.

16 The contrary motive impelled Hoover to organise the sending of *American* grain to Germany (see Lochner, 38 ff.). Woodrow Wilson had the same idea (R. S. Baker, II, 323). Only Radek evaded the German ban on the entry of the delegation. He describes the journey and his highly interesting encounters with a number of German political and military leaders in the article in *Krasnaya Nov* referred to above, note 11.

[17] A. Korsunski, 'Rapallski Dogovor i Nemetskaya Sotzial-Demokratiya', *Voprosi Istorii*, No. 8, 1950, 119.   The same argument is adduced in Ya. Tsitovitch, 'O roli S.Sh.A. v spasenii Germanii ot polnovo razgroma v 1918 godu' (*Ibid*. No. 12, 1950).

[18] House Papers, IV, 121.

[19] It is even possible that the very date of the Armistice was determined in part by this fear. On the eve of the signature of the Armistice, for example, Field-Marshal Sir Henry Wilson describes this scene at a Cabinet meeting: 'Lloyd George read two wires from Tiger describing Foch's interview with the Boches, and Tiger is afraid that Germany will break up and Bolshevism become rampant. Lloyd George asked me if I wanted this, or would rather have an armistice, and I unhesitatingly said "armistice". All the Cabinet agreed.   Our real danger now is not the Boches but Bolshevism' (Callwell, II, 148). It was consistent therefore of Wilson, and also of Milner, to object to German demobilisation on the grounds that 'Germany may have to be the bulwark against Russian Bolshevism'. Wilson would only agree to German disarmament 'as to field artillery and machine-guns, but would let the Germans withdraw with the honours of war, i.e. drums beating, colours flying and infantry armament' (House Papers, IV, 118).

[20] Terrail, 234.

[21] *Ibid*. 243-9.

[22] *Ibid*. 258. Curiously enough, although it was in a somewhat distorted form, Lenin had wind of the purport of these discussions only two or three days after they had taken place. This is what he told the Sixth Extraordinary Congress of Soviets on November 6th: 'We know that they (i.e. the Anglo-French imperialists) have overwhelmed the Wilson government with the request that German troops be left in Poland, the Ukraine, Esthonia and Livonia, because, although they are enemies of German imperialism, these troops are serving their purpose: they are suppressing the Bolshevists. Let them go only when ententeophile "troops of liberation" appear in order to crush the Bolsheviks!' (Lenin, XXVIII, 129). In fact, certain of the more forward-looking German circles were, from August 1918 onwards, envisaging co-operation with the Allies on the basis of the *status quo* in the West, combined with an anti-Bolshevik policy in the East (cf. Fritz Fischer, 849-54).

[23] Erzberger, 332; see also *ibid*. 334.

[24] *Ibid*. 337.

[25] The evolution of Article XII and the comments of the German delegation can best be followed in Der Waffenstillstand, ed. Marhefka, I, 36-9. In the light of the foregoing it is difficult to dismiss the influence of Bolshevism on the Armistice terms as summarily as does Wheeler Bennett, for example—see his *Nemesis of Power*, 40, n. 3. Erzberger was carrying out a policy later defined by Stresemann as 'representing' German policy 'from the point of view of a struggle against Bolshevism' (Stresemann, *Diaries*, II, 185). As regards the final version of Article XII, *The Times* (October 27th, 1919) explained that the Allies hoped to use the German army of occupation in Eastern

Europe 'as a protection for Western Europe against the Bolsheviks and did not stipulate for an immediate evacuation, as there were no local forces considered capable of making head against Bolshevik aggression'.

26 See note 19 above.

27 Max von Baden, 580. Listen again to Scheidemann: 'My party will see to it that Germany is saved from Bolshevism' (ibid. 618).

28 Chicherin (3), 22.

29 Lenin, XXVIII, 129.

30 Tanin, 40.

31 Scheidemann, 224 ff.

32 Ebert, II, 103-4. Cf. the following judgement: 'After the November Revolution the Social Democratic Party . . . and its smaller off-shoot, the Independent Social Democratic Party . . . formed a government that made earnest efforts to remodel Germany along Western lines and to accommodate Allied wishes. The Socialist ministers carried out the exceptionally severe terms of the Armistice, turned a cold shoulder to pariah Soviet Russia, and showed deference and even pusillanimity to France's protégé, Poland' (Wm. Maehl, 'The German Socialists and the Foreign Policy of the Reich from the London Conference to Rapallo', *Journal of Modern History*, No. 1, March 1947). It is also interesting to note that Erzberger, Minister without Portfolio in charge of Armistice affairs in the new Cabinet formed with Scheidemann as Chancellor, proposed to hand over the imprisoned Bolshevik, Radek, to the Allies. This was part of the policy of currying favour with the West. But Brockdorff-Rantzau, non-party Foreign Minister and later, as German Ambassador to Russia, one of the foremost supporters of a pro-Russian policy, frustrated this attempt (Epstein, 290; Helbig, 17-18).

33 R. S. Baker, II, 64.

34 Cf. Lloyd George's memorandum: 'The greatest danger that I see in the present situation', he wrote in a memorandum offered to the Peace Conference in March 1919, 'is that Germany may throw in her lot with Bolshevism and place her resources, her brains, her vast organising power at the disposal of the revolutionary fanatics whose dream it is to conquer the world for Bolshevism by force of arms. . . . If we are wise, we shall offer to Germany a peace which, while just, will be preferable for all sensible men to the alternative of Bolshevism' (Cmd. 1614, 1922). Smuts suffered from the same fear. Also in a memorandum for the Peace Conference he pointed to the danger that only the Bolsheviks would gain an advantage should Germany be 'destroyed' by a harsh peace treaty; and Smuts, therefore, concluded that German 'appeasement now may have the effect of turning her into a bulwark against the on-coming Bolshevism of eastern Europe' (Hancock, *Smuts, The Sanguine Years*, 510-12). Such views were by no means uncommon in the British delegation at Versailles (ibid. 514).

35 D.B.F.P. First Series, II, No. 47, 25.

36 They provoked from the adviser on Russian political affairs in the

German Foreign Office the following comment: 'Germany is to be prevented from acquiring any influence in or over Russia that might contribute to the political or economic recovery of Germany. Therefore, any approach of Germany to Russia is to be made as difficult as possible and the shaping of the mutual relationship of both countries is to be made completely dependent on the wishes and needs of the Allied powers. . . . Simultaneously, the Allies wish to reserve to themselves later the right of exercising a decisive influence over the whole political and economic future of Russia as well as its constitutional (*staatsrechtlich*) structure' (Zitelmann, 2-3); cf. also the verdict on Articles 116 and 117 as being 'conceived and formulated in the intention of creating an abyss between Germany and the hoped for non-Bolshevik Russia of the future and of keeping Russia and Germany apart' (F. T. Epstein, 'Zur Interpretation des Versailler Vertrags', *Jahrbücher für Geschichte Osteuropas* 3, V, 1957).

[37] Mantoux, I, 461; see also Hölzle, 81, and F.R.U.S. Paris Peace Conference, 1919, XIII, 273.

[38] See note 93, p. 106 below.

[39] F.R.U.S. etc. VI, 845, 951.

[40] D.B.F.P. First Series I, No. 19, 207.

[41] D.B.F.P. First Series, II, No. 56, 744-6.

[42] *Ibid*. No. 62, 782.

[43] This transition is studied in E. Birke, 'Die französische Osteuropapolitik 1914–1918', *Zeitschrift für Ostforschung*, 3, III, 1954; see also Hölzle, 85.

[44] Jules Cambon, 'La Paix—notes inédites, 1919', *Revue de Paris*, November 1st, 1937. Namier (*Conflicts*, 25-6) points out that 'If a new order was to be secured in East-Central Europe it could not be against all the Great Powers east of the Rhine. . . . No system can be permanently maintained on the European continent east of the Rhine which has not the support either of Germany or of Russia, especially if its other guarantors are not anxious to exert themselves.' A number of mutual conflicts further intensified the weakness inherent in the various components of the *cordon sanitaire*. Did Vilna belong to Lithuania or Poland? Was the Teschen area to fall to Poland or to Czechoslovakia? These were two typical bones of contention. Also, the strength of the *cordon* suffered from the divided and contradictory attitude of its two chief patrons. There were many cases—Eastern Galicia and Upper Silesia, for example—where Polish aggrandisement was encouraged by France and thwarted by Britain.

[45] *Izvestiya*, November 5th, 1925.

[46] Lenin, XXX, 355.

[47] The note of triumph in Lenin's voice must be seen in the context of Allied, especially French, efforts to continue to use these states as a means to enforce the isolation of the Soviets. Berthelot, French Minister of War, for example, told an inter-Allied conference in London on February 19th, 1920, that 'in his opinion it was imperative that the Border States should definitely be told that they would drop out of the Alliance and be subjected to the same treatment as Soviet Russia

should they have any independent dealings with the Soviet Government'. (D.B.F.P. First Series, VII, No. 16, 142.) As for the use of Poland as a *place d'armes* for attacks on Russia, Millerand, President of the Council, had this to say: 'He had personally advised M. Patek [Polish Foreign Minister] . . . against making peace with the Soviets. . . . If the Council endorsed the advice that he had given personally to M. Patek and counselled Poland to reject the peace offer [i.e. from the Soviets], it would be necessary for the Powers to give some degree of assistance and support to that country against Russia. She was especially in need, for example, of 150,000 Mauser rifles.' But this proposal showed the Anglo-French divergence, for Lloyd George refused to add 'a single farthing to [Britain's] already heavy load of debt in order to help Poland, should she continue the war' (*ibid*. No. 22, 196, 202).

48 Protokolli IX Syezda R.K.P. (b), 5.

49 Kochan, 14-16. An eye-witness report is of interest. The Chief of the Mission to the Baltic Provinces reported from Libau in June 1919: 'We are all of us intensely apprehensive over the results of the present policy of drift which is inevitably leading these countries under complete German control. Yet without the presence of the German forces there would be complete anarchy and Bolshevism. . . . I do not believe that Paris realises the gravity of the situation. We have left these border countries either to Bolshevism or Germanism; whichever proves strongest. At present Germany is consolidating her position here and looks to Russia to recoup from this war' (F.R.U.S. Paris Peace Conference, 1919, III, 199).

50 D.B.F.P. First Series, I, No. 41, 501-2; No. 67, 824-5 and App. G., 830.

51 The German note is reported in *The Times*, October 31st, 1919. (The reference to the blockade is not to the wartime measure that lasted until May 1919 but to the Allied blockade of the German Baltic coast, imposed in order to accelerate the return of the German troops.)

52 Verhandlungen des Reichstags, CCCXXX, 3359 ff.

53 D.B.F.P. First Series, II, No. 7, 8.

54 *Ibid*. Nos. 27, 30, 51, 58, 86.

55 Bainville, 'L'Allemagne', 223 (article published in November 1918 in *L'Action Française*).

56 D.B.F.P. First Series, VI, Nos. 82, 84, 104, 105.

57 *Ibid*. IX, No. 23.

58 *Ibid*. No. 552. To Lord d'Abernon, who became British Ambassador in Berlin at the end of 1920, the French demand for the total disarmament of the *Einwohnerwehr* (an armed volunteer organisation) was 'almost insane'. 'The French do not appear to understand,' he commented, 'that the military danger point is past and that the real danger in Germany is communist disorder' (d'Abernon, I, 87). British tenderness towards German unofficial right-wing military formations was long-lived and is evident in a most revealing report from Colonel (later General Sir) John Marshall-Cornwall, the British Military Attaché in Berlin, 1928–32. 'The Stahlhelm', he writes in December 1931, 'as a patriotic organisation has much to commend it, and one

cannot help feeling that most decent Britons, were they Germans of today, would be Stahlhelmers. The movement, which originally developed out of a defensive league of property-owners against Spartacist revolutionary outbreaks formulates a sane patriotism with the idea of consolidating the orderly elements of society against Bolshevik ideas. It combines an association of war veterans, akin to the British Legion, with a younger branch of higher military potential, which may be likened to something between our Boy Scouts and Territorial Army' (D.B.F.P. Second Series, II, App. IV, 520).

⁵⁹ See above, p. 16.

⁶⁰ Lenin, XXXI, 281. See also Zetkin, 20-1. Churchill, who writes that 'Poland was the linch-pin of Versailles', endorses Lenin's view (*The World Crisis—The Aftermath*, 261); so does General von Seeckt, the first Chief of the *Reichswehr*: he saw in the collapse of Poland the end of 'the most essential aims of the policy of Versailles' (Gessler, 185).

⁶¹ D.B.F.P. First Series, VIII, No. 83; cf. also Kilmarnock to Curzon on July 22nd, 1920: 'Perhaps the most serious danger with which we are confronted is that of a close understanding or even alliance between Germany and Russia' (*Ibid.* X, No. 180, 276).

⁶² Protokolli X Syezda R.K.P. (b), 271.

⁶³ Churchill, *op. cit.* 270.

⁶⁴ See the following articles by Radek: *Zur Taktik des Kommunismus*, Berlin, 1919; 'Die auswärtige Politik des deutschen Kommunismus und der Hamburger National-Bolschewismus', *Die Internationale*, 17-18, December 20th, 1919; *Die auswärtige Politik Sowjet-Russlands*, Hamburg, 1921 (written December 1919); 'Deutschland und Russland', *Die Zukunft*, No. 19, February 7th, 1920. Something of the same realism had already been evident in Litvinov's remarks to the Webbs, 'He is pessimistic about the Russian Revolution', noted Beatrice Webb in January 1918. 'Unless capitalism is overthrown in other countries the Russian Revolution will not survive. If European militarism does not destroy it, economic pressure will. The catastrophe must be universal, or the superior efficiency of "bourgeois government" will make the "proletarian" government appear a failure!' (Webb, 106).

⁶⁵ Lenin, XXXI, 251.

⁶⁶ *Ibid.* 301.

⁶⁷ Verhandlungen des Reichstags, CCCXIV, 766-7.

⁶⁸ D.B.F.P. First Series, X, No. 193, 288. Lord d'Abernon, on the spot as a member of the Allied Mission to Warsaw, found that the German ban on the transport of munitions, following the declaration of neutrality, made 'the question of how to get munitions through to Poland from the West one of immense difficulty' (Lord d'Abernon, *The Eighteenth Decisive Battle of the World*, 48); see also D.B.F.P. First Series, XI, No. 473, 517.

⁶⁹ Hilger, 50; see also Radek in *Pravda*, October 15th, 1921.

⁷⁰ E.g. Millerand, the French Premier, told an Allied conference of the danger 'that Germany wished to profit by Poland's adversity in order to get back in the east what she had lost in the west; that is to

say, that she would seek to get Posen or Upper Silesia' (D.B.F.P. First Series, VIII, No. 83, 712). Churchill noted that 'the reactionary Germans would of course be delighted to see the downfall of Poland at the hands of the Bolsheviks for they fully understand that a strong Poland standing between Germany and Russia is the one thing that will baulk their plans for reconstruction and revenge' (Churchill, *op. cit.* 265). To Beneš, the then Foreign Minister of Czechoslovakia, 'one thing was sure, that Germany would endeavour to draw all the profit she could for herself. If she came to the rescue of Poland, that country would henceforth be entirely under German domination. But if Germany allowed Poland to be crushed it would mean a prior understanding with the Bolshevik Government and the beginning of a Russo-German alliance' (D.B.F.P. First Series, XI, No. 210, 236).

It is worth noting at this point Bismarck's view of an independent Poland. He compared it to 'the creation of an ally for any enemy who might attack us. A sovereign Polish state with an army of its own would be, as it were, a French camp on the Vistula, with 100,000 to 150,000 good troops ready to attack us in the rear, if we should have to defend ourselves in the West' (Rothfels, *Bismarck und der Staat*, 117).

[71] Chicherin (3), 31.

[72] Lenin, XXXI, 444 ff.

[73] Blücher, 144.

[74] Hilger, 66-7; Helbig, 47. Other evidence to this effect is summarised in Freund, 84-5. The military collaboration eventually led to the establishment in Russia of a number of arms, poison gas and aeroplane factories and of training grounds for the German Army (see Speidel, 'Reichswehr und Rote Armee', *Vierteljahrshefte für Zeitgeschichte*, I/I, January 1953). Further material on this topic is contained in Gatzke, 'Russo-German Military Collaboration during the Weimar Republic', (*American Historical Review*, LXIII, No. 3, April 1958) and in Carsten, 'The Reichswehr and the Red Army' (*Survey*, No. 44-5, October, 1962). This development is an ironic comment on Chicherin's denial of 1919: ' . . . the Red Army with its extremely well developed revolutionary spirit would be quite unable to have anything to do with the products of the old German military system' (*Soviet Russia*, November 8th, 1919). Chicherin had forgotten that *raison d'état* conquers all.

[75] Verhandlungen des Reichstags, CCCXLVI, 1994.

[76] Maisky, 103.

[77] Helbig, 51-2.

[78] Verhandlungen des Reichstags, CCCLI, 4736.

[79] See Günter Rosenfeld, 'Das Zustandekommen des Rapallo-Vertrags', *Zeitschrift für Geschichtswissenschaft*, IV, 4, 1956, 680; Hilger, 74.

[80] Helbig, 56 ff.

[81] Stein, 249.

[82] *Izvestiya*, November 27th, 1921.

[83] Gessler, 191.

[84] Maisky, 107.

H

[85] Gessler, 191-2.
[86] A point emphasised by Stein, 319 ff.
[87] Rathenau, *Cannes und Genua*, 17-18.
[88] See Poincaré, IV, 198-9, for his extremely suspicious attitude towards the proposed conference. He would only support it on condition that disarmament and reparations were excluded from the agenda.
[89] D'Abernon, I, 238.
[90] Verhandlungen des Reichstags, CCCLII, 5562.
[91] See his remarks in *Izvestiya*, January 28th, 1922.
[92] Archives of Büro des Reichspräsidenten, quoted Rosenfeld, *op. cit.* 684. This is phrased slightly differently in Protocol of the Council of Ministers of April 5th, 1922 (quoted Zimmermann, 113-14). Rathenau is speaking: 'The Russians now wanted to discuss everything conceivable with us. How far we would support Russia would depend on the degree of its accommodation (*Entgegenkommen*). We would come to terms with Russia in this but must avoid thereby coming into conflict with the Western Powers.'
[93] Article 116 of the Treaty of Versailles played a certain part in hastening the conclusion of the Rapallo agreement. The possibility, however remote, that Russia might claim reparations from Germany strengthened the hand of those members of the German delegation who favoured the attainment of a unilateral agreement with Russia which would annul all such claims. The German reparations expert at the Genoa Conference, Carl Bergmann, compared Article 116 to a sword of Damocles hanging over Germany (Bergmann, 126).
[94] Protokolli II Syezda R.K.P. (b), 12.
[95] Koblyakov, 7-8.
[96] Chicherin in *Izvestiya*, April 16th, 1924.
[97] *Ibid.* April 21st, 26th, 1922.
[98] *The Times*, April 20th, 1922.
[99] Cmd. 1667, 1922, 53-4.
[100] Parliamentary Debates, House of Commons, Fifth Series, Vol. 154, cols. 1457-8, May 24th, 1922.
[101] See above, note 34, p. 101.
[102] From a speech at Bar-le-Duc reported in *The Times*, April 25th, 1922.
[103] Quoted Selsam, 54, n. 25.

III—A WESTERN COUNTER-BLOW

[1] Gessler, 239.
[2] K. Radek, *The Winding up of the Versailles Treaty*, Report to the Fourth Congress of the Communist International (Eng. trans. Hamburg, 1922), 16.
[3] d'Abernon II, 238.
[4] Documents, ed. Degras, I, 369.
[5] Cmd. 1943, 1923.
[6] Hilger, 120; see also Gessler, 239 and Fischer, 452.
[7] *Izvestiya*, January 24th, 1923.

8 Documents, ed. Degras, I, 376. (But Trotsky remained confident that the attack would not in fact be launched.)

9 Gessler, 239; see also Schmidt-Pauli, 124.

10 This much at least emerges from Höltje, 38-41, who quotes various reports from the German Ambassadors in Warsaw and Prague and also sundry circulars of the German Foreign Office.

11 See his remarks on this subject Protokolli XIV Syezda R.K.P. (b), 660-1.

12 *Izvestiya*, April 16th, 1924.

13 Protokolli XV Konferentsii V.K.P. (b), 30.

14 d'Abernon III, 119.

15 Stresemann, *Essays and Speeches*, 143.

16 For all the above see Clay, 212-13.

17 *The Scotsman*, October 3rd, 1924.

18 Note, for example, the following jottings by Stresemann : 'If we do not attain co-operation with the financially powerful states, with America, which in these questions is on the side of Britain and France, then I foresee an economic collapse of Germany . . .' (Stresemann, *Vermächtnis*, II, 149 dated July 17th, 1925); 'It seems as though a sort of Anglo-American-German capital trust is being formed which naturally has as presupposition the conclusion of the Security Pact. We need those milliards very urgently.' (*Ibid.* II, 154, July 19th, 1925.) It was also made clear to Stresemann by Benjamin Strong, the Governor of the Federal Reserve Bank, that, if the German negotiations with the Western powers were to fail through German opposition, there would be no U.S. loans (*ibid.* II, 222). President Coolidge enthusiastically welcomed the Locarno agreements as 'a step towards peace'. In his message to Congress in December 1925 he said it was 'exceedingly gratifying to observe this progress, which both in its method and in its results promises so much that is beneficial to the world' (F.R.U.S. 1925, I, XII-XIII). This whole point is well analysed in A. Thimme, 'Die Locarno-Politik im Lichte des Stresemannschen Nachlasses', *Zeitschrift für Politik*, 3/1, 1956.

19 Article 16 was one of the 'sanctions' Articles. In view of its tremendous importance in all Germany's subsequent negotiations with Russia and with the Western powers, it is given here in full:

'Should any Member of the League resort to war in disregard of its covenants under Articles 12, 13 or 15, it shall *ipso facto* be deemed to have committed an act of war against all other Members of the League, which hereby undertake immediately to subject it to the severance of all trade or financial relations, the prohibition of all intercourse between their nationals and the nationals of the Covenant breaking state, and the prevention of all financial, commercial or personal intercourse between the nationals of the Covenant breaking state and the nationals of any other State, whether a Member of the League or not.

'It shall be the duty of the Council in such case to recommend to the several Governments concerned what effective military, naval or air force the Members of the League shall severally contribute to the armed forces to be used to protect the Covenants of the League.

'The Members of the League agree further that they will mutually support one another in the financial and economic measures which are taken under this article, in order to minimise the loss and inconvenience resulting from the above measures, and that they will mutually support one another in resisting any special measures aimed at one of their number by the Covenant breaking state, and that they will take the necessary steps to afford passage through their territory to the forces of any of the Members of the League which are co-operating to protect the Covenants of the League.

'Any Member of the League which has violated any Covenant of the League may be declared to be no longer a Member of the League by a vote of the Council concurred in by the representatives of all the other Members of the League represented thereon.'

[20] d'Abernon, III, 151.

[21] E.g. Reynaud, I, 48, and Turok, 6.

[22] *Izvestiya*, November 5th, 1925.

[23] Protokolli XIV Syezda V.K.P. (b), 652-3.

[24] *Ibid.* 16.

[25] *Izvestiya*, November 5th, 1924.

[26] Hilger, 179; Helbig, 134.

[27] The speeches on this occasion are reported in *Izvestiya*, November 22nd, 1924. Krassin emphasised that the nub of the question was the provision of German long-term credits.

[28] Dirksen, 57.

[29] Stein, 239-40.

[30] Documents, ed. Degras, I, 463.

[31] This was Rykov's theme, in a speech reported in *Izvestiya*, November 28th, 1924.

[32] These talks are described in Z. Gasiorowski, 'The Russian Overture to Germany of December 1924', *Journal of Modern History*, XXX, No. 2, June 1958, 100-2.

[33] Carr, 81.

[34] GFM2/4562/154922-30; see also Hilger, 138 and n. 4. (Herbette was the recently-appointed first French Ambassador to the Soviets.)

[35] Rakovsky, 23-4. This is, of course, the precise contrary of the later Soviet thesis of the 'indivisibility of peace'.

[36] Protokolli Zasedanii Tsik Sovetov, 2 Sozyv, 3 Sessiya, 33.

[37] Petrie, II, 254; d'Abernon, III, 155 (editorial note). This argument was also put forward in the House of Commons by the historian H. A. L. Fisher: '. . . if England were to enter into an exclusive pact with France and Belgium we should, in effect, be initiating a process which would ultimately and inevitably lead to the division of Europe into two groups of powers arrayed against one another. . . . We all know that one of the first answers which would be made to such a triple alliance of the Western powers would be a combination between Russia and Germany. . . .' (Parliamentary Debates, House of Commons, Fifth Series, Vol. 181, col. 695, March 5th, 1925.) Another historian, Sir James Headlam-Morley, the then Historical Adviser to the

Foreign Office, wrote in similar and prophetic terms: 'It is the real interest of this country to prevent a new alliance between Germany and Russia, an alliance which would no doubt be cemented by an attack on Poland' (*Studies in Diplomatic History*, 183).

[38] d'Abernon, I, 20-2.

[39] Parliamentary Debates, House of Commons, Fifth Series, Vol. 188, col. 441, November 18th, 1925.

[40] Sir A. Chamberlain to Sir George Grahame (British Ambassador in Brussels) February 26th, 1925. Chamberlain's reluctance to make more use of this argument is explained in certain remarks he made to M. Skirmunt, the Polish Ambassador in London: 'What I had said to him was not that I desired to detach Germany from Russia, but that I desired to avoid throwing Germany into the arms of Russia by repelling her from the society of the Western nations. This was a matter of interest and importance to us all, but the less we spoke of it in public, the better it would be, for the German Nationalist opposition to the policy of agreement with the Allies perverted this argument into a suggestion that our only object in making the pact was to embroil Germany with Soviet Russia and use her as a cat's paw to pull the chestnuts out of the fire for us. I had no doubt, however, that the strongest reason of Germany for hesitation about entering the League, was the opposition and the threats of Russia' (Sir A. Chamberlain to Max Muller, British Ambassador in Warsaw, July 28th, 1925). These letters are taken from the Chamberlain Papers in the University of Birmingham Library and are quoted by kind permission of the Trustee, Mr. K. W. Humphreys.

[41] Quoted Suarez, VI, 137. Note also Briand's statement to the *Petit Parisien* (February 26th, 1927): 'Aujourd'hui, que voyons-nous?' he asked rhetorically; and he answered: 'Une Allemagne résolument tournée vers l'Occident, en dépit de ses accords avec la Russie; une Allemagne qui a compris enfin que son véritable intérêt était de s'entendre avec les Alliés et particulièrement avec la France.' 'Briand knew,' it has been stated, 'that the major success of Locarno was prevention of a German–Russian combination . . . .' (Wandycz, 367). But this did not prove to be the case, as will be shown below.

[42] d'Abernon, I, 20.

[43] Petrie, II, 280.

[44] Schmidt, 83. See also below, p. 44.

[45] Stresemann, *Nachlass*, GFM2/7131/148289 ff.

[46] The above is based on the minutes of the conference kept by Dirksen (Stresemann, *Nachlass*, GFM2/7319/160067 ff.). The document is available in an English translation in *International Affairs* (Moscow), No. 7, 1956, pp. 155-62. An invaluable Soviet publication —*Lokarnskaya Konferentsiya*, ed. Dobrov et al., Moscow, 1959—contains the text of the notes (in Russian translation) made by the secretary of each delegation of the proceedings of the conference, German, French, British, Italian and Belgian.

[47] d'Abernon, III, 147.

[48] *Vermächtnis*, II, 246.

⁴⁹ Petrie, II, 259. On June 27th, 1928, in reply to a Commons question, Chamberlain again repudiated any notion of further commitments or guarantees by Britain (Parliamentary Debates, House of Commons, Fifth Series, Vol. 219, col. 509). But as a counter-balance to the unhappy forecast cited above and in fairness to Chamberlain it must be added that, like Churchill, he later made a complete *volte-face*. He even gave an interview to *Pravda* (quoted *Morning Post*, March 27th, 1935), in which he declared that there was no doubt about the necessity of the co-operation of Soviet Russia in any complete system of European security. 'If war breaks out anywhere it is impossible to predict how far it may spread. Security in Eastern and Central Europe is no less essential than security in Western Europe.'

⁵⁰ Petrie, II, 268.

⁵¹ Z. Gasiorowski, 'Stresemann and Poland after Locarno', *Journal of Central European Affairs*, XVIII, No. 1, 42.

⁵² *Vermächtnis*, II, 553-5; see also *ibid*. 172. One of the few contemporary foreign observers to comprehend the dynamic nature of German foreign policy was, curiously enough, Stalin. In his report to the Party Congress at the end of 1925 he emphasised that Germany 'was growing and advancing' and to suppose that it would reconcile itself to its post-Versailles frontiers was 'to count on a miracle. If previously, after the Franco-Prussian war, the Alsace-Lorraine question . . . served as one of the most important causes of the imperialist war, then what guarantee is there that the Versailles peace and its continuation—Locarno, which legalises and juridically consecrates Germany's loss of Silesia, the Danzig Corridor and Danzig, the loss of Ukrainian Galicia and Western Volhynia, the loss of the Western part of Byelorussia—what guarantee is there that this treaty which has made mincemeat of a whole series of states and created a whole series of knots of contradictions, will not share the fate of the old Franco-Prussian Treaty which tore Alsace-Lorraine from France after the Franco-Prussian War? There is not and there cannot be any such guarantee' (XIV Syezda V.K.P. (b), 13-14).

⁵³ Stresemann, *Nachlass*, GFM2/7133/148390. A shorter version in *Vermächtnis*, II, 513-14.

⁵⁴ *Ibid*. GFM2/7415/175580 ff.

⁵⁵ *Ibid*. GFM2/7129/147857 ff.

⁵⁶ *Vermächtnis*, II, 109.

⁵⁷ This document is reprinted in Schieder, 91, and in Höltje, 247.

⁵⁸ The document containing this interchange is reprinted in K. D. Erdmann, 'Das Problem der Ost- oder Westorientierung in der Locarno-Politik Stresemanns', *Geschichte in Wissenschaft und Unterricht*, 6/3, March 1955, 153 ff.

⁵⁹ Rakovsky, 43; Chicherin in *Izvestiya*, October 4th, 1925.

⁶⁰ Stockhausen, 176.

⁶¹ Dirksen, 68.

⁶² As was recognised, for example, by Schurman, the American Ambassador in Berlin. 'It does seem', he telegraphed to the State Department, 'that Chicherin is by all odds the best bargaining card that the

Germans hold, and I gather that Luther and Stresemann mean to play it for all it is worth' (quoted F. E. Hirsch, 'Stresemann in Historical Perspective', *The Review of Politics*, XV, No. 3, 374).

[63] Fischer, 604.

[64] See above, p. 44.

[65] *Izvestiya*, April 25th, 1926.

[66] Parliamentary Debates, House of Commons, Fifth Series, Vol. 194, col. 1190, April 21st, 1926; see also d'Abernon, III, 249. d'Abernon himself is described as being 'deeply concerned' at the conclusion of the pact (GFM2/4562/156857).

[67] GFM2/7415/175547.

[68] GFM2/4562/157518 ff.

[69] GFM2/7415/175551 ff. The Germans, in their reply to the French and British protests, asserted that the German undertakings entered into *vis-à-vis* Russia were 'declaratory affirmations' and not 'contractual obligations'. Stresemann agreed with this line (GFM2/4562/157455-6).

[70] *The Times*, October 26th, 1925.

[71] This vindicated a prophecy made by Sir Robert Hodgson, the British Chargé d'Affaires in Moscow, a much more perceptive observer than d'Abernon. Hodgson denied that 'Germany's signing the pact of security and entering the League would make any violent difference in Russo-German relations' (d'Abernon, III, 191).

[72] It might even be said that Locarno actually tended to bring Russia and Germany together; for, by putting the German eastern frontier on a lower status than the western, it encouraged German revisionism to move eastwards. But, as Stresemann said, the solution of the Corridor question was 'hardly conceivable without the co-operation of Russia and Germany' (GFM2/4556/149432).

[73] The inexpediency, from the Western standpoint, of a neutralised Germany, has recently been emphasised by Dr. Adenauer. It would mean, he said, 'the end of Germany . . . it would strengthen the position of the Soviet Union and would lead to a change in the balance of power in Europe and in the world' (*The Times*, July 14th, 1961). The same point has been made by Mr. McInnis, who writes: 'The fact is that even for Russia, and still more for the west under present conditions, German neutrality is a poor second choice. It is preferable to a Germany actively aligned with the opposing bloc; it is not a substitute for a Germany attached as a firm ally' (McInnis, 161).

[74] Dirksen, 75. (I have amended slightly the English translation.)

[75] *Vermächtnis*, II, 61.

[76] *League of Nations Armament Year Book*, Third Year, Geneva 1927, 480.

[77] This despatch is reproduced in full in Höltje, 254-6.

[78] Z. Gasiorowski, 'Stresemann and Poland after Locarno' (*Journal of Central European Affairs*, XVIII, 3, October 1958), describes the interchange on this occasion; see also Hilger, 158, n. 8.

[79] *Bulletin of International News*, IV, No. 25, June 9th, 1928. This whole policy once again was the direct contrary of the later policy of collective security, indivisibility of peace, etc.

[80] Leninism, II, 325.

[81] Schmidt, 134.

[82] Documents of the Preparatory Commission of the Disarmament Conference, Series V, Minutes of the 4th Session, 14-15. Litvinov called Russo-German collaboration at Geneva not 'Zusammcnarbeit' but 'Parallelarbeit' (GFM2/1841/419301).

[83] Vermächtnis, III, 113.

[84] Helbig, 197.

[85] Vermächtnis, III, 150-1.

[86] Rykov, 48-50.

[87] Dirksen, 80; Fischer, 774-80. It is significant, for example, that Boris Stein, the chief Soviet delegate at Geneva, should question the German Consul there as to the reason for the Russian exclusion (GFM2/1842/419542-3).

[88] Documents of the P.C.D.C., Series VIII, Minutes of the Sixth Session, 1st Part, 25.

[89] Documents, ed. Degras, II, 447.

IV—THE LONDON-BERLIN AXIS

[1] Parliamentary Debates, House of Commons, Fifth Series, Vol. 281, cols. 50-1, November 7th, 1933.

[2] Vermächtnis, II, 523.

[3] Ibid. III, 65.

[4] Morgan, I, 240; François-Poncet, 146. Flandin comments bitterly (Politique française 1919–1940, 46, n. 1): 'En réalité, le rapport final de la Commission de contrôle, après avoir énuméré en 504 pages toutes les difficultés qu'elle avait rencontrées dans sa mission, toutes les infractions de l'Allemagne, concluait que l'Allemagne n'avait jamais désarmé ni eu l'intention de désarmer; et que, pendant sept ans, elle avait fait tout ce qui était en son pouvoir pour contrecarrer la commission dans l'exercice de son contrôle. Le rapport fut "étouffé" d'un commun accord entre MM. Briand et Austen Chamberlain, qui laissèrent entendre que les résultats du contrôle final de désarmement allemand avaient été satisfaisants, ce qui permit à la commission d'admission, chargée d'examiner la requête de l'Allemagne à la S.D.N., de déclarer que l'Allemagne ayant rempli ses obligations internationales, rien ne s'opposait à son admission à Genève.'

[5] One of the professional diplomats noted that 'there was no change in foreign policy except that more emphasis was to be placed on support of the League of Nations' (Kirkpatrick, 41).

[6] Vermächtnis, III, 556-7.

[7] Parliamentary Debates, House of Commons, Fifth Series, House of Commons, Vol. 229, col. 416, July 5th, 1929. (This had earlier been recommended by Chamberlain, ibid. col. 406.)

[8] But Curtius refused to make a 'Dankesbesuch' to Briand (Curtius, 137).

[9] D.B.F.P. Second Series, I, No. 332, 525.

¹⁰ *Ibid.* No. 309, 489.

¹¹ *Ibid.* No. 317, 501, n. 5. This was an early example of the later differences between the Foreign Office and its political head. It was followed up in March 1934 by a Foreign Office memorandum which argued that 'the old question of French security must now be viewed, not merely as hitherto in its generalised form as part of an international convention on Armaments, but in its more concrete form as an ingredient in the future organisation of British security against the impending menace created by Germany's uncontrolled rearmament' (D.B.F.P. Second Series, VI, No. 363, 579).

¹² D.B.F.P. Second Series, VII, No. 579, 667.

¹³ *Mezhdunarodnaya Zhizn*, No. 3, 1929, 37-50.

¹⁴ *Pravda*, December 5th, 1929; for further evidence of deterioration in Russo-German relations at this time see GFM2/1842/419775.

¹⁵ Verhandlungen des Reichstags, CCCCXXVIII, 5817; cf. also: '. . . Every political movement in Germany seemed to have some reason for anger and resentment against the Soviet Union. The Nationalist Right seized upon the treatment of the German-speaking population, the anti-religious campaign, and the open sympathy of Moscow with civil war and revolt in Germany, the moderate left was indignant over the venom poured out over the government parties by the Soviet press. A general press campaign against Soviet politics set in throughout Germany, in which every single "incident" was given sensational treatment' (Hilger, 229). See also Dirksen, 97.

¹⁶ Both issues dated March 15th, 1930.

¹⁷ *Mezhdunarodnaya Zhizn.* No. 3, 1930, 3-18. This is one of the very few references to the impact of the First Five Year Plan on the Soviet diplomatic position. It is impossible to say anything precise on this point beyond the fact that such a tremendous shift in industrial power was bound to have diplomatic repercussions. A contemporary German view is of interest. Schubert, Staatssekretär in the German Foreign Office, is talking to Sir Horace Rumbold in June 1930: 'The real danger would come later,' he said, 'supposing the Soviet Government were able to put through their five-year industrial plan and their agricultural scheme. . . . If they did, Europe would have to be prepared for the dumping of Russian goods on a large scale. She would have to protect herself against this proceeding. Moreover, the success of the Five-Year Plan etc., would be convincing propaganda for the Soviet system' (D.B.F.P. Second Series, VII, No. 89, 142).

¹⁸ See above, p. 53.

¹⁹ Hilger, 233-4. 'Brüning', writes Dirksen, 'avoided any initiative in that direction [i.e. of Moscow] and any support which he did give was confined to a bare minimum' (Dirksen, 112); see also Hilger, 250.

²⁰ Dirksen, 113. Hilger adds: 'lest French nationalist opinion be aroused' (Hilger, 251).

²¹ Dirksen, 76-7. It was also symptomatic that the German Foreign Office held aloof from the visit to Russia of a most important group of German industrialists in February/March 1931 (Dirksen, 105; Hilger, 241).

²² For details see Kochan, 163.
²³ D.B.F.P. Second Series, VII, No. 139, 215.
²⁴ Weizsäcker, 91; see also Dirksen, 114, and Curtius, 248.
²⁵ GFM2/1538/375204-5; *ibid*. 1882/424883-4, 424893, 425024.
²⁶ D.G.F.P. Series C, I, No. 6, 14.
²⁷ *Ibid*.
²⁸ *Izvestiya* commented, for example (May 6th, 1933). 'Whilst welcoming the prolongation of the Berlin Treaty, Soviet public opinion fully realises that treaties have that meaning with which the concrete practical activity of the contracting parties endows them.'
²⁹ The details of this scheme are not clear but its salient features are to be found in Herriot, II, 338-9, 345, 347; Papen, 198 ff.; Laroche, 109, and D.G.F.P. Series C, I, No. 43, n. 2, 91.
³⁰ It is noteworthy, for example, that Nadolny, who followed Dirksen as German Ambassador to Moscow in October but only stayed there until June 1934, had not only opposed Germany's withdrawal from the League and the Disarmament Conference but also sought to pursue a policy of friendship with Russia. (See in particular D.G.F.P. Series C, II, No. 476, 860-7.) He had not realised that the German aim of securing concessions in the West excluded a simultaneous pro-Russian policy. This was the consequence to Hitler's discarding of Stresemann's policy of balance. See Rahn, 83-4, and Nadolny, 141, 167-9, where Hitler explained that 'he wanted to walk with England and to have nothing to do with Russia'.
³¹ D.G.F.P. Series C, I, No. 29, 620. Both Dirksen (115) and Coulondre (167) point to 1931 as the year of Russia's turning away from Germany. The impact of the projected Union can be judged from the tone of Russian Press comment. It was treated by *Izvestiya* (March 24th, 1931) as a symptom of the increasing self-assertion of German capitalism against France, as a German reply to Briand's Pan-Europa scheme. It would increase German pressure on Poland and Czechoslovakia and bring Germany into economic contact with Italy, Yugoslavia and Hungary with inevitable political consequences. Radek (*Izvestiya*, May 1st, 1931) also saw the Customs Union as a sign of expansionism—in fact, he argued, it was only to the south that Germany could expand at all. Eastwards and westwards the way was barred by France. But the projected *Anschluss*—which was what in fact the Customs Union amounted to—denoted a return to the idea of *Mitteleuropa*.
³² Documents, ed. Degras, II, 473.
³³ *Ibid*. 478.
³⁴ D.B.F.P. Second Series, VII, No. 143, 218.
³⁵ See above, p. 51.
³⁶ *Izvestiya*, November 22nd, 1931.
³⁷ Documents, ed. Degras, II, 518.
³⁸ Brüning in the Reichstag Foreign Affairs Committee, May 24th, 1932 (quoted Höltje, 177-8). The Russo-Polish non-aggression pact did in fact contain no guarantee of the Polish frontiers, in contradistinction to some of the other Russian non-aggression pacts, e.g. the one with Finland. None the less, Brüning had hit on a *point névralgique*. How-

ever much he disliked the Russians, it was still impossible to 'solve' the Polish problem without Russian co-operation. This had earlier been noted by Stresemann (see above p. 111, note 72). It would be acted on by Hitler in 1939.

[39] Dirksen, 116.

[40] Stalin, 32-4; Litvinov, 87 ff.; Molotov, 484-5.

[41] Seeckt, 45.

[42] Meinck, 149.

[43] D.G.F.P. Series C, II, No. 390, 733-4.

[44] D.B.F.P. Second Series, VI, No. 488, 814; see also *ibid.*, No. 496, 832. 'Naturally', Simon said on another occasion, 'entry into an eastern guarantee and security system with the obligation to render mutual assistance, was out of the question for England' (D.G.F.P. Series C, II, No. 502, 901).

[45] D.G.F.P. Series C, III, No. 102, 202.

[46] Flandin, Premier at the time, told the Chamber on February 25th, 1936, that 'dès le début la conception d'une alliance analogue à celle d'avant la guerre avait été résolument écartée' (Journal Officiel, Débats Parlementaires, No. 20, 580). Leger, Secretary-General at the Quai d'Orsay, told Ribbentrop quite correctly that the pact had become bi-lateral solely 'through the development of circumstances' (D.G.F.P. Series D, IV, No. 370, 476). This had not been part of the original French plan. For further evidence of the weakness of the pact and French hostility to association with Russia see also Churchill I, 105-6; Reynaud I, 115 ff.; Micaud, 68 ff.; D.G.F.P. Series D, III, No. 66, 67.

[47] D.B.F.P. Second Series, VII, No. 582, 670. Note also Simon's letter to Chamberlain in August 1934: 'We should not ourselves pro-pose Russia for membership . . . but we must be prepared to support the proposal when made by others. . . . I should very much like to make our approval of Russia's candidature dependent upon the fulfil-ment by Russia of some conditions e.g., the settling of the Lena Gold-fields matter or stopping Communist propaganda' (*ibid.* No. 609, n. 1, 711).

[48] Quoted Young, 223. At this time also Baldwin was 'not indisposed' to forming an alliance with Hitler 'to form a bulwark against the spread of Communism' (Jones, 209).

[49] Jones, 231.

[50] Documents and Materials, I, No. 1, 24.

[51] See Hitler's 'Memorandum on the Tasks of a Four-Year Plan' in *Vierteljahrshefte für Zeitgeschichte* April II/3, 1955, 204 ff.

[52] Documents and Materials, I, No. 1, 19-20. Chamberlain, said Sir Horace Wilson, had been 'particularly pleased' by Hitler's comparison of England and Germany as 'two pillars upon which the European social order could rest' (D.G.F.P. Series D, I, No. 148, 271). This was also the view of Geoffrey Dawson, then editor of *The Times* (Wrench, 362). Dirksen could therefore logically link Anglo-German understanding with an anti-Russian policy. The British government of 1936 'which had made agreement with Germany one of the major points of its programme . . . has come nearer to understanding the

most essential points of the major demands advanced by Germany, with respect to excluding the Soviet Union from the decision of the destinies of Europe, the League of Nations likewise, and the advisability of bilateral negotiations and treaties' (Documents and Materials, II, No. 4, 34).

Halifax also introduced a pamphlet by Lord Lloyd, a prominent appeaser, containing these remarkable passages. Lloyd describes the Russo-German pact as 'Herr Hitler's final apostasy. It was the betrayal of Europe.' But until then—'The need for order and discipline in Europe, for strength at the centre to withstand the incessant infiltration of false and revolutionary ideas—this is certainly no more than the conventional excuse offered by every military dictator who has ever suppressed the liberties of his own people or advanced to the conquest of his neighbours. Nevertheless, so long as it could be believed that the excuse was offered with sincerity, and in Herr Hitler's case the appearances of sincerity were not lacking over a period of years, the world's judgment of the man remained more favourable than its judgment of his actions. The faint possibility of an ultimate settlement with Hitler still, in these circumstances remained. However abominable his methods, however deceitful his diplomacy, however intolerant he might show himself to the rights of other European peoples, he still claimed to stand ultimately for something which was a common European interest, and which therefore could conceivably provide some day a basis for understanding with other nations equally determined not to sacrifice their traditional institutions and habits on the bloodstained altars of the World Revolution.

'The Conclusion of the German-Soviet pact removed even this faint possibility of an honourable peace' (Lord Lloyd, The British Case, 53-5).

⁵³ Jones, 185; Coulondre, 153: see also Beloff, I, 108-10. Litvinov saw, most convincingly, the explanation of the appeasement policy not in diplomacy or foreign policy 'but rather in the social-political sphere; not in national but in class policy . . . there are not a few people among the governing classes of western countries who naively believe that fascism is really a solid barrier against an advance by the working class. And since the aggressor states are at the same time the bulwark of fascism, they fear that a defeat of the aggressor states in a war, or even their diplomatic defeat, might prove to be a defeat for fascism . . . To this is added one more apprehension, that for the necessary balance in the struggle against the aggressor countries, co-operation with the Soviet Union is essential, and this, it appears, might also have repercussions upon the domestic political struggle. Thus it appears these reactionary circles prefer to sacrifice their national interests, to endanger and even lose their state positions for the sake of preserving their social and class positions' (Documents, ed. Degras, III, 291-2). This is certainly borne out by the position in France (Coulondre, 35-6, 148. See also Paul-Boncour, III, 153-4). Alexandrovsky, the Russian envoy in Prague, took a corresponding view of Beneš: 'I do not doubt', he wrote to Narkomindel in September 1938, 'that this dry pedant and

hard-bitten diplomat from the very outset has been pinning all his hopes and still does, on obtaining the maximum possible assistance for Czechoslovakia by relying on Britain and France, and regards assistance from the USSR to defend Czechoslovakia against an attack by Hitler as an extreme suicidal measure for the Czechoslovak bourgeoisie. . . . I explain Beneš' behaviour as springing from the same social fear that grips and actuates the other "appeasers" in Europe. Beneš is afraid of the masses. Formerly he often and even willingly said that if the worst came to the worst he would appeal to the people and the people would support him, while of late he has begun to fear the people' (New Documents, No. 56, 124-5). The conclusion that Beneš 'would not go it alone with Russia . . . [and] opted quite deliberately, yet inevitably, for the west' is reached in W. V. Wallace, 'The Foreign Policy of President Beneš in the Approach to Munich' (*Slavonic and East European Review*, Vol. 39, 1960–61). As for Chamberlain, his former Parliamentary Private Secretary, Lord Home, has explained that he 'saw Communism as the major long-term danger. He hated Hitler and German Fascism, but he felt that Europe in general and Britain in particular were in even greater danger from Communism' (*The Observer*, September 16th, 1962).

54 *The Observer*, April 23rd, 1961. Wheeler-Bennett (*Munich*, 295-6) comes to a similar conclusion: 'behind the general desire for peace and for an "accommodation" with Hitler there lay, if not in the mind of Mr. Chamberlain himself at any rate in the minds of some of his advisers, the secret hope that, if German expansion could be directed towards the East, it would in time come into collision with the rival totalitarian imperialism of Soviet Russia. In the conflict which would ensue both the forces of National Socialism and Communism would be exhausted. . . .'

55 D.G.F.P. Series C, III, No. 468, 887. Lothian also favoured 'a coalition of the democracies to block any German move in their direction and to turn Germany's course eastwards. That this might lead to a war between Russia and Germany does not seem to disturb him seriously' (Dodd, 249); see also Butler, *Lothian*, 335.

56 Documents and Materials, I, No. 44, 300-1 (italics in the original).

57 D.G.F.P. Series D, IV, No. 286, 362 and No. 287, 367. Kennedy, the American Ambassador, reported in the same sense: 'Chamberlain does not take the possibility of a Russian-German alliance seriously. He says that they are both so distrustful of each other that it would never work out; and that it is Hitler's hope of course to stir up enough trouble in the Ukraine so that he can point out how badly the Russians are treating the Ukrainians and that he could go in if he wanted to and in this way get some more concessions without any strain on his resources' (quoted Langer, 60). Langer himself comments: 'It is probably safe to assume that news of friction between Germany and Poland was taken everywhere in the West as a welcome promise that Hitler would turn his attention eastward' (*ibid.*). See also Kennedy's report of February 20th, 1939: 'My observations, and I have talked with Chatfield, Simon, Hoare, Halifax and Chamberlain, in addition to

many other people, are that they thoroughly believe that England is on
its way; that Germany will not attack; that the problem of last fall,
when they were obliged to do things that perhaps they would rather
have done otherwise, is gone, and that while England will not go to
war if Germany should attack Rumania or Ukraine, they would declare
war at once if Germany moved towards Switzerland or Holland' (quoted
Tansill, 449). The possibility of German disruption in the Ukraine
had already provoked Chamberlain to remark that it would be 'unfor-
tunate if France should one day find herself entangled as a consequence
of her relations with Russia' (D.B.F.P. Third Series, III, No. 325,
306-7).

58 Whitaker, 267.
59 Documents on International Affairs, 1938, I, 315.
60 Evidence to this effect is assembled in Duroselle, 57.
61 Coulondre, 42, 45.
62 Byrnes, 283; F.R.U.S. Conferences at Malta and Yalta, 925.
63 GFM2/1538/375256.
64 Ibid. 375276.
65 Ibid. 1906/429107. Kandelaki, a Georgian, claimed to have close
personal relations with Stalin and Molotov. At the beginning of 1937
the German Foreign Office checked this assertion with the Embassy
in Moscow. It was fully confirmed by Schulenburg, who reported to
Berlin that Kandelaki 'enjoys the confidence of Stalin' (GFM2/1907/
429293-4).
66 Ibid. 429147-50.
67 Ibid. 1907/429299-300.
68 Documents, ed. Degras, III, 153-5.
69 Ibid. 173-4.
70 Ibid. 184. In the summer of 1938 an American correspondent in
Moscow was allowed to inform his journal in the following terms of
certain supposed steps being taken by Germany to improve its relations
with the Soviet Union: 'Any such initiative on the part of the German
Government which would contribute to the cause of world peace would
probably meet with success, but that if not directed to this end would
be considered by the Soviet Government as an attempt to break the
democratic front'. 'His wording', writes Kirk, the American Chargé
d'Affaires in Moscow, 'was suggested by the censor himself and therefore may be taken as reflecting the considered opinion of the Soviet
Foreign Office' (F.R.U.S. Soviet Union, 1933-39, 584-5. See also
D.G.F.P. Series D, I, No. 626, 920-1).
   At this time also a speech on the international situation made by
Litvinov was thought by Schulenburg to contain 'remarkably little
aggressiveness and [it] strives to leave open all possibilities. The attempt
to arrive at an objective attitude towards the policy of the Third Reich
is striking' (ibid. No. 627, 924).
71 GFM2/1907/429296. According to Krivitsky (I was Stalin's Agent,
38-9), Kandelaki returned from Berlin to Moscow in April 1937 with
the draft of a Russo-German agreement from which Hitler later withdrew. But there is no documentary evidence for this.

[72] Parliamentary Debates, House of Commons, Fifth Series, Vol. 333, col. 1406, March 24th, 1938. At this time Chamberlain suffered from the fear that Russia was attempting to involve Germany and Britain in hostilities: '. . . our Secret Service', he wrote, darkly, 'doesn't spend all its time looking out of the window . . .' (quoted Feiling, 347).

[73] D.G.F.P. Series D, II, No. 266, 434 and No. 290, 486. Chamberlain was in fact thinking at this time of an Anglo-French-German-Italian pact, excluding Russia (Beloff, II, 130, n. 2); see also D.G.F.P. Series D, I, No. 146, 262 and No. 148, 272.

[74] Davies, 194.

[75] Weizsäcker circular of August 22nd, 1939, quoted Beloff, Soviet Studies, II, 2, 136-7.

[76] This is all based on Schulenburg's most interesting despatch of December 3rd, 1938 (D.G.F.P. Series D, V, No. 108, 138-40).

[77] Coulondre, 167.

[78] Quoted above, p. 111, note 72.

[79] See above, p. 73.

[80] Coulondre, 171.

[81] D.B.F.P. Third Series, IV, No. 121, 124. The same note had been struck by a Pravda article as early as September 21st, 1938. 'The Soviet Union examines with composure the question which particular imperialist robber stretches out his hand for this or that colony or vassal state, for it sees no difference between German and English robbers.'

[82] Hilger, 288-9; Kordt, 155, n. 2. Whatever the precise status of this arrangement may have been, it is to be noted that Hitler's references to Bolshevism in his Nuremberg speech in September 1938 were considerably less aggressive than the previous year (cf. Baynes I, 688 ff. and 712 ff.). Of equal note, both for its absence of personal polemics and its mention of a second imperialist war was Molotov's speech on the anniversary of the Bolshevik Revolution on November 6th. But if an imperialist war was in progress was there any reason why the Soviet Union should discriminate between the Beelzebub of Fascism and the devil of 'the so-called democracies'? This does not apparently follow. Although Molotov denounced British and French readiness to sacrifice Czechoslovakia 'for the sake of an agreement with the aggressors', they themselves, he infers, were not aggressors. His reaction was to reiterate Russia's reliance on its own strength as the guarantee of peace (Documents, ed. Degras, III, 308-11).

This sort of long-range dialogue was continued with Hitler's speech of January 30th, 1939; it was marked by a noteworthy absence of any hostile reference to the Soviet Union. In fact in a speech devoted largely to foreign affairs there was barely a mention of Russia (cf. Baynes, II, 1567). For an interesting Czech and French evaluation of the speech in the sense of an impending Russo-German agreement see D.B.F.P. Third Series, IV, No. 69, 64, and No. 76, 71). The importance of analysing the war as 'imperialist' is brought out in a report from the British Embassy in Moscow on February 20th, 1939: 'In the event of a European war, there is every reason to suppose that the attitude of the Soviet Government would . . . be one of nervous neutrality and that the principal aim of Soviet policy would be to prevent the Soviet Union from itself becoming involved. . . . It is perhaps worth mentioning that such an attitude has been justified in advance by the Soviet press, which consistently refers to the impending struggle as the "Second Imperialist War" with which the mighty Soviet Union, safe behind its own frontiers, need not be concerned' (D.B.F.P. Third Series, IV, App. III, 611-12).

[83] D.G.F.P., Series D, IV, No. 492, 627.
[84] *Ibid.* No. 495, 631.
[85] D.B.F.P. Third Series, IV, No. 76, 71.
[86] International Military Tribunal, XXXIV, 381, Doc. 120-C.
[87] Degras, III, 315-22.
[88] F.R.U.S. Soviet Union 1933-39, 748-9. Stalin himself later affirmed that it had been his intention with this speech to improve relations with Germany (Gaus's affidavit International Military Tribunal XL, 297, Doc. Hess, 16; Ribbentrop, 180). Of course, as has been pointed out (e.g. *The World in March 1939*, 531), the inherent ambiguity of Stalin's speech is such that it could claim to anticipate and promote either of two contradictory tendencies). Molotov, a few months later, said the speech 'which had been well understood in Germany—had brought about the reversal in political relations' (N.S.R., 76). Ribbentrop himself went a long way to confirm this impression in including the speech amongst 'certain signs that Soviet views were tending towards' a new orientation (D.G.F.P. Series D, VI, No. 441, 590).
[89] D.G.F.P. Series D, IV, Nos. 236-7, 275-6. The reason for the German renunciation is given in a draft of Ribbentrop's instructions to Schulenburg towards the end of May. He points out that the time is opportune for a normalisation of Russo-German relations; he points to the toning down of press polemics as earnest of German desire to achieve this. He goes on: 'If this should be regarded in Moscow merely as temporary tactics, attention should be drawn to the tangible fact that, for example, our attitude towards the question of the Carpatho-Ukraine and our leaving it to Hungary shows that we are completely devoid of expansionist intentions over the Ukraine' (D.G.F.P. Series D, IV, No. 441, 590). It is not certain that this despatch was actually sent but that does not affect its import; cf. also Weizsäcker's memorandum of a conversation with the Russian chargé in Berlin: '. . . Beck's interpretation of the German policy towards the Ukraine was refuted by the German conduct in the case of the Carpathian-Ukraine' (N.S.R., 14).
[90] Kleist, 27-8; N.S.R. No. 1, 1-2; Assmann, 93-4.
[91] N.S.R., 3.
[92] D.B.F.P. Third Series, I, No. 229, 315.
[93] Documents on International Affairs, 1939-46, I, 446. In a letter to Mussolini of August 25, Hitler also wrote: 'The readiness on the part of the Kremlin to arrive at a reorientation of its relations with

Germany, which became apparent after the departure of Litvinov . . .'
(N.S.R., 81).

[94] Hilger, 296-7; Kleist, 37-8.

[95] N.S.R., 6.

[96] International Military Tribunal, XXXVII, 550; Doc. 079-L

[97] Such is the irony of history that this reversal of rôles made the despised Chamberlain, in the end, redeem his earlier guilt. It was, after all, Chamberlain who declared war on Hitler—at a time when Stalin's own essay in appeasement matched anything attained by Chamberlain.

[98] Strang, 161; see also D.G.F.P. Series D, VI, No. 154, 191. It was drafted in order to reply to a Parliamentary question concerning any measures the British government would take should there be an imminent German attack on Poland.

[99] D.B.F.P. Third Series, V, No. 4, 23.

[100] Parliamentary Debates, House of Commons, Fifth Series, Vol. 345, col. 2482.

[101] In this debate it does not seem that the Russians attached much importance to the first choice. Stalin simply did not consider the British 'bündnisfähig'. He told Alanbrooke that he 'thought England must be bluffing; he knew we had only two divisions we could mobilise at once, and he thought we must know how bad the French Army was and what little reliance could be placed on it. He could not imagine we should enter the war with such weakness. On the other hand, he said he knew Germany was certain ultimately to attack Russia. He was not ready to withstand that attack; by attacking Poland with Germany he could make more ground, ground was equal to time and he would consequently have a longer period to get ready' (Bryant, 472). Another reason for the the failure of the Anglo-Russian negotiations may perhaps lie not so much in the fact that both parties to the negotiations were also simultaneously seeking agreement with Germany, but rather in the unfounded Russian suspicion that Britain looked on the negotiations as a means to embroil Russia in a war with Germany. A recent Soviet history writes as follows: 'The negotiations were to demonstrate the isolation of the Soviet Union in its confrontation with fascist aggression and in this way to push Germany into an attack on the Soviet Union. By the threat of an alliance with the U.S.S.R., the governments of Britain and France strove to force Germany to enter into a far-reaching agreement with them which would not hamper the interests of British and French monopolies on the world markets and would ensure an attack by Germany on the U.S.S.R.' (Pospelov, 163).

[102] Templewood, 383. Dirksen called it 'twin action policy' ('Zwillingspolitik'). 'England wants by means of armament and the acquisition of allies to make herself strong and equal to the Axis, but at the same time she wants by means of negotiations to seek an adjustment with Germany, and is prepared to make sacrifices for it; on the question of the Colonies, raw material supplies, Lebensraum, and spheres of economic interest' (Documents and Materials II, No. 29, 176). The

I

Russian counterpart to Templewood's analysis was formulated by Astakhov in Berlin in June. He told Draganov, the Bulgarian minister, that there were three courses open to Russia: the western pact, spinning out the negotiations, or a *rapprochement* with Germany. The last of these was 'closest' to Russian desires (N.S.R., 21).

[103] D.G.F.P. Series D, VI, No. 716, 980.

[104] D.B.F.P. Third Series, VI, No. 533, 580-1.

[105] Documents and Materials II, No. 24, 118. Dirksen, to whom the above proposals were made on August 3, comments: 'The dominant feeling was that compared with an effective adjustment with Germany, the ties that had been formed in the last few months with other powers were only a subsidiary means which would cease to be operative as soon as agreement with Germany, the all-important objective worth striving, for, had been really attained' (*ibid.* 124); for further evidence concerning Chamberlain's desire for an accommodation between Germany and Poland, involving sacrifices by the latter, and Chamberlain's disbelief in the feasibility of an understanding with Russia, see *Ironside Diaries*, 77-8.

[106] Documents and Materials II, No. 29, 187.

[107] D.G.F.P. Series D, VI, No. 716, 980-3. Much the same programme of Anglo-German economic co-operation was also propounded by Hudson, Secretary of the Department of Overseas Trade, in a conversation with Wohltat (D.B.F.P. Third Series, VI, No. 370, 407-10).

V—DIPLOMACY BECOMES WAR

[1] Ivanov, 63-4.

[2] See, e.g., G. L. Rosanov's 'Die Pläne zur Aufteilung Deutschlands während des zweiten Weltkrieges und ihre Behandlung in der reaktionären Geschichtsliteratur' in *Probleme der Geschichte des Zweiten Weltkriegs*, ed. Leo Stern, Berlin, 1958, 227-37.

[3] Churchill, III, 472-3.

[4] *Ibid.* 558-9.

[5] F.R.U.S. 1942, Europe, III, 517-18.

[6] *Ibid.* 520; see also Woodward, 191 ff.

[7] *Ibid.* 542.

[8] *Ibid.* 510. 'To defer decision, while a matter of principle, was also a device of diplomacy', most aptly comments the State Department historian (Feis, 59).

[9] Hull, II, 1170. It was prescient of the Foreign Office to argue that 'The President is unduly optimistic in supposing that some other form of security in lieu of the reoccupation of the Baltic States will prove acceptable to M. Stalin' (F.R.U.S. 1942, Europe, III, 525).

[10] Churchill, IV, 304.

[11] *Bolshevik*, No. 10, May 1942.

[12] A fact made clear by Litvinov, for example, to Harry Hopkins in March 1943. (Sherwood, II, 710.)

[13] The position was further complicated by differing conceptions of

political warfare and, in 1943, by a certain crisis of confidence between the Allies. As to the first, there was a world of difference between the Western policy of unconditional surrender—itself part of the *tabula rasa* policy of avoiding commitments—and that embodied in Stalin's famous declaration of 1942: '. . . It would be ludicrous to identify Hitler's clique with the German people, with the German State. The experience of history indicates that Hitlers come and go, but the German people and the German State remain' (*Great Patriotic War*, 27). Thus, Stalin deprecated talk of unconditional surrender (Hull, II, 1572 ff.; Sherwood, II, 777). He himself used the term only once—in his Order of the Day for May 1, 1943: 'Is it not clear', Stalin asked rhetorically, 'that only the utter routing of the Hitlerite armies and the unconditional surrender of Hitlerite Germany can bring peace to Europe?' (*Great Patriotic War*, 58). Later, of course, faced with the deliberate German policy of extermination and massacre in Russia, it became increasingly impossible to maintain the fiction of a Nazi clique dominating a German people. Towards the end of 1943 the tone of Stalin's pronouncements changed: and a year later a Soviet writer, Yovchuk, even wrote: 'The population of Germany, which is responsible for the crimes of the Hitlerite clique can only re-acquire the right to be included in the ranks of the peoples of Europe by years of intense effort and rigorous trials'. (*Bolshevik*, No. 22, November 1944). This article is referred to again below, p. 126, note 60.

[14] See above, p. 80.

[15] Churchill, IV, 717-18. This, too, is the theme of certain remarks made by Churchill to Smuts, a few months later. Taking as his *point de départ* the inevitability of Russia's emergence from the war as 'the greatest land power in the world', Churchill hoped for an association of British and United States power that 'may put us on good terms and in a friendly balance with Russia at least for the period of re-building' (Churchill, V, 115). Smuts himself at this time, with the same aim of providing a balance against Russia, was thinking in terms of a closer association between the Commonwealth and the nations of Western Europe. France, Belgium, Holland, Norway and Denmark would acquire something in the nature of Dominion status in the Commonwealth (cf. Smuts' speech to the Empire Parliamentary Association on November 25th, 1943, in Documents and Speeches on British Commonwealth Affairs, 1931-52, ed. Mansergh, I, 568 ff.).

The idea of confederations as part of the answer to the problem of post-war European security goes back to the end of 1941 when the Foreign Office had urged the necessity of a confederation of Poland and Czechoslovakia and of the various Balkan States (F.R.U.S. 1941, I., General, The Soviet Union, 203). Later it was hoped that Soviet approval of this principle would serve as part of the *quid pro quo* for Anglo-American recognition of the Russian conquests in the Baltic. (*Ibid.* 1942, Europe, III, 516-17).

If any further confirmation were needed that 1943 saw the birth of the post-war political situation it comes from Hitler. 'As our difficulties mount', he told a naval conference in August 1943, 'the conflicting objectives of the Allies increase and become more evident. Maisky and Litvinov have been recalled unexpectedly [they were the Russian Ambassadors in London and Washington]. . . . There is danger of an expansion of Russian power into the heart of Europe. I have no doubt whatsoever that the Anglo-Saxons are still ruthlessly bent upon our annihilation. Actually the British have manoeuvred themselves into an awkward position. They entered the war in order to "preserve the balance of power" in Europe. Meanwhile Russia has awakened and, from the viewpoint of technological and material advancement, developed into a great power. . . . Only if all of Europe is united under a strong central power, can there be any security for Europe. . . . That means that in the future the challenge of the East can be met only by a Europe united under German leadership. This will be to the advantage of Britain also' (Führer Conferences on Naval Affairs 1943, 85-6, 9-11 August 1943).

[16] Woodward, 439, 441; Sherwood, II, 709, 711.

[17] Hull, II, 1233-4. The State Department report is contained in Department of State Publications, No. 3580, Postwar Foreign Policy Preparation, Washington, 1950.

[18] Hull, II, 1265-6.

[19] Welles, 336-61.

[20] F.R.U.S. The Conferences at Cairo and Teheran, 1943, 600-1.

[21] Sherwood, II, 711.

[22] Hull, II, 1288-9. The Russians, reported Harriman from Moscow after the Foreign Ministers' Conference, 'are determined to have no semblance of the old "cordon sanitaire" concept in eastern Europe' (F.R.U.S. Conferences at Cairo and Teheran, 1943, 154).

[23] Bolshevik, No. 1, January 1944.

[24] Voina i Rabochii Klass, No. 14, July 15th, 1943.

[25] Ibid. No. 11, June 1st, 1944.

[26] Ibid. No. 15, August 1st, 1944.

[27] F.R.U.S. Conferences at Cairo and Teheran, 1943, 846 (italics added).

[28] Hull, II, 1255-6.

[29] F.R.U.S. Conferences at Malta and Yalta, 612; cf. also ibid. 624. 'Without intending to do so,' it has been said of the consequences of the zonal system, 'the wartime allies had taken the first step towards the present partition of Germany' (Snell, 57).

[30] Mosely, 168. At one stage the Americans also opposed the allocation of separate zones of occupation (Woodward, 442).

[31] Strang, 218. But it is also interesting to note that certain British military opinion also rejected 'mixed zones' as 'administratively impracticable' (Morgan, 124). Eisenhower proposed an Anglo-American zone but this 'had possible political implications that negatived its acceptance' (Hull, II, 1613).

[32] Early in the planning of the Second Front, it was in any case accepted that 'the Russian zone would naturally be the affair of the Russians . . .' (Morgan, 123).

[33] Leahy, 252.
[34] Mosely, 169–70.
[35] *Ibid.* 171.
[36] Strang, 207.
[37] See above, p. 93.
[38] Mosely, 167, 171.
[39] Strang, 218.
[40] *Ibid.*
[41] Yalta Papers, 128–9. 'At a time', writes Winant's economic adviser, 'when an important conference was to begin at Quebec in a few days, when the allied armies were entering Germany, and other enemy resistance in Europe might collapse at any time, the President had not made up his mind on what should be done with Germany after the war, and the four highly placed advisers whom he had designated to help him were hopelessly divided. One of them wished to wreck Germany's industries and flood her mines, a second wished to prohibit her from manufacturing her most essential industrial materials, a third wished to eliminate her economic power and keep her people at a subsistence level, and a fourth was left to struggle for a human and statesmanlike attitude' (Penrose, 254). The four advisers were respectively Morgenthau, Hopkins, Hull and Stimson; cf. also Dorn, adviser to the U.S. Military Governor in Germany, 1945–47: 'The fact remains that a sustained effort to negotiate a common occupation policy before the end of the war was not made, and when it was made at the Potsdam Conference it was too late' ('The Debate on American Occupation Policy in Germany in 1944/5', *Political Science Quarterly*, LXXII, December 1957, 489); cf. also Sherwood, II, 835.
[42] F.R.U.S. Conferences at Malta and Yalta, 158–9.
[43] Hull, II, 1620–1.
[44] Sherwood, II, 804.
[45] Strang, 206.
[46] Churchill, VI, 210.
[47] Stettinius, 158.
[48] F.R.U.S. Conferences at Malta and Yalta, 627. (Italics in the original.) Some measure of Churchill's opposition to the idea of dismemberment may be gauged from the formidable array of hazards that he massed against it. He argued that it 'would require elaborate searchings by experienced statesmen on the historical, political, economic and sociological aspects of the problem and prolonged study by a sub-committee' (*ibid.* 612).
[49] *Pravda*, May 10th, 1945.
[50] Byrnes, 26: at Potsdam even Stalin agreed that dismemberment was now considered 'inadvisable' (F.R.U.S. The Conference of Berlin, 1945, II, 522).
[51] Truman, I, 223.
[52] F.R.U.S. The Conference of Berlin, 1945, II, 61.
[53] *Ibid.* I, 50–1.
[54] *Ibid.* II, Doc. No. 1027, 1000–1.
[55] *Ibid.* I, Doc. No. 399, 587. The same consideration applied to any

separation of the Ruhr and/or the Rhineland. This, wrote Stimson, Secretary for War, would 'tend to drive the industries which formerly were dependent upon the Ruhr and the Rhineland to look to Eastern Germany and Poland. I think there would be a strong tendency to drive Germany towards the East in her economic affiliations and outlook. I do not think that is in the interests of either Western Europe or the United States' (*ibid*. II, Doc. No. 1022, 991). It was also doubted by Mosely, political adviser to Winant, whether a small West German state, minus the Ruhr, would be able 'to withstand the pull' exerted by a greater East German state (*ibid*. Doc. No. 1023, 993).

⁵⁶ *Ibid*. II, 522.

⁵⁷ This expression is used in Mosely, 154.

⁵⁸ Churchill, V, 623.

⁵⁹ Churchill, VI, 63 ff., 198 ff.

⁶⁰ Ehrman, 55. The Russian press made no secret of the Soviets' revolutionary aims: cf. *Bolshevik*, No. 22, November 1944: 'In order to avoid, in the post-war period, the repetition of the mistakes of the past, the freedom-loving peoples must not only utterly destroy all the sources which have nourished fascism, but they are obliged to paralyse the activity of the pro-fascist elements in allied and neutral countries'.

⁶¹ Stettinius, 60.

⁶² Churchill, VI, 388 ff.; Leahy, 391 ff.

⁶³ *Ibid*. p. 388, cf. also Churchill, VI, 389. 'He [i.e. Eisenhower] feared that if the Russians were brought into a question of the surrender of Kesselring's forces what could be settled by himself in an hour might be prolonged for three or four weeks, with heavy losses to our troops. He made it clear that he would insist upon all the troops under the officer making the surrender laying down their arms and standing still until they received further orders, so that there would be no possibility of their being transferred across Germany to withstand the Russians.'

⁶⁴ Leahy, 417. But there were, of course, Soviet representatives present when the terms of surrender were accepted by the Germans.

⁶⁵ Churchill, VI, 390-1.

⁶⁶ *Ibid*. 407.

⁶⁷ *Ibid*. 442.

⁶⁸ *Ibid*. 446 ff.

⁶⁹ *Ibid*. 389.

⁷⁰ Montgomery, 232-3; Pogue, 488; see also Churchill, VI, 449, where Churchill also emphasises the importance of an American push to the region south of Stuttgart where the main German atomic research installations were concentrated.

⁷¹ Ehrman, 159-60; Deane, 159-60; Pogue, 504-5. This Allied renunciation has been perversely described by a Russian historian as the destruction by the Red Army of 'the plan of the American imperialists for the seizure of Prague and the occupation of Czechoslovakia . . .' (Deborin, 364). It is of note that the planning for the Second Front had originally excluded both Poland and Czechoslovakia from its scope (Morgan, 127).

⁷² Churchill, VI, 397.

V—DIPLOMACY BECOMES WAR 127

[73] Speidel, 90-1, 118. Goerdeler himself looked forward to a détente with the western powers which would make it possible 'to concentrate all the military forces of the German people in the east' (Ritter, 590). With no apparent sense of incongruity Professor Ritter, the foremost apologist of the German resistance, writes: 'The greatest fear of the German patriots was the invasion of Central Europe by the Red Army. Was it not in fact the greatest danger for Europe as well? Was not the Western alliance with the totalitarian régime of the East unnatural, only entered into because of the dire necessity to destroy Hitler's tyranny first? Would there not then arise the possibility of concluding a quick peace with the West and of stopping the Russian advance on the Polish frontier? Would not the German resistance movement then be fulfilling a European mission?' (Gerhard Ritter, *The Political Attitude of the German Army 1900–1944* in *Studies in Diplomatic History*, ed. Sarkissian, 345).

[74] Köller, 39-40.

[75] Bernadotte, 105-17.

[76] Dönitz, 145. This viewpoint was echoed in German propaganda, as witness this extract from a broadcast made by William Joyce on April 28th, just before Dönitz took over from Hitler: '. . . If Berlin falls, Europe will fall with it. . . . In these critical days the Fuehrer has taken the major decision that, whatever else happens, the available strength of the Reich shall be concentrated on the attempt to prevent the Bolshevik flood from rolling westwards. This is not merely a German but a European decision. . . . It is indeed a ghastly and obscene irony that the men who are defending the Western world against the mighty hordes from hither Asia should be stabbed in the back by the Western democracies. . . .' (The transcript of this broadcast was kindly placed at my disposal by the B.B.C.)

[77] Dönitz, 434.

[78] Ocherki, 476; another Soviet source writes that the Germans had on the whole 800 kilometres of the Western front only 35 'incomplete divisions of limited fighting capacity' (Deborin, 348).

[79] Dönitz, 449.

[80] *Ibid.* 451.

[81] Lüdde-Neurath, 434 (*Das Ende auf deutschem Boden*).

[82] Eisenhower, 464. It is because of this contrast perhaps that an East German historian comments that 'Eisenhower's loyalty to the alliance by no means included that of his subordinates' (D. Zboralski, 'Zur Geschichte der Zusammenarbeit anglo-amerikanischer Kreise mit der geschlagenen faschistischen Armee und die Versuche deren Kader zu retten', 224, in *Probleme der Geschichte des Zweiten Weltkriegs*, ed. Leo Stern).

[83] Lüdde-Neurath, 76; who estimates that the 9 days of the Dönitz régime's delaying tactics enabled 'two and a half to three million Germans [to be] saved from the Russians'.

[84] Schultz, 87-8. The author was a member of the operational department of the Wehrmachtführungsstab in the last month of the war.

[85] Lüdde-Neurath, 75.

[86] See, e.g., Israelyan, 306.

[87] The nearest approach to the reality of such co-operation was Churchill's order to Montgomery at the very end of the war not to disarm the surrendering German troops lest they be needed to fight the Russians. So much for the solemn pledges to disarm Germany! *Raison d'état*, once again, conquers all. 'I telegraphed to Lord Montgomery', Churchill told his constituents, 'directing him to be careful in collecting the German arms, to stack them so that they could easily be issued again to the German soldiers whom we should have to work with if the Soviet advance continued' (*The Times*, November 24th, 1954).

[88] But since Soviet generals, by contrast with their British and American colleagues, have produced no worth-while memoirs, we have no precise knowledge of such objectives.

[89] It has even been suggested by Churchill that the bringing forward of this offensive, originally scheduled for the second half of May, was provoked by the unexpectedly swift approach of the Allied armies to the Elbe (Churchill, VI, 441).

[90] Of course, the frontiers that emerged in the confusion of combat were not yet final. The Americans ended the war in occupation of a large sector of the Soviet Zone. This resulted from an earlier miscalculation on the part of Churchill and Roosevelt. Churchill explained that at the time the Zones were defined 'it was not foreseen that General Eisenhower's armies would make such a mighty inroad into Germany' (Truman, I, 63-4).

[91] Leonhard, 256-7.

[92] Kleist, 235-84, especially 241, 266.

[93] Stalin, 50.

[94] Kleist, 243.

[95] Sherwood, II, 709.

[96] See, e.g., Strang, 200; Leahy, 148-9, 177, 222; Churchill, VI, 444.

[97] Quoted from Mikolajczyk's private files in Rozek, 247.

BIBLIOGRAPHY

1. DOCUMENTS

Cmd. 1667, 1922; Cmd. 1943, 1923.

Der Waffenstillstand 1918–19. Das Dokumentenmaterial, 3 vols., ed. Marhefka, Berlin, 1928.

Documents and Materials Relating to the eve of the Second World War, 2 vols., Moscow, 1948.

Documents and Speeches on British Commonwealth Affairs, 1931–52, 2 vols. ed. Mansergh, Oxford, 1953.

Documents on British Foreign Policy (D.B.F.P.): First Series, Vols. I, II, VI, VII, VIII, IX, X, XI; Second Series, Vols. II, VI, VII; Third Series, Vols. IV, V, VI.

Documents on German Foreign Policy (D.G.F.P.): Series C, Vols. I, II, III; Series D, I, II, III, IV, V, VI.

Documents on International Affairs, 1938, Vol. I; 1939–46, Vol. I.

Documents on Russian Foreign Policy, 3 vols., ed. Degras, Oxford, 1951–53.

Documents Réunis: La Guerre entre les Alliés et la Russie 1918–20, ed. Moulis, E., and Bergounier, E., Paris, 1937.

Foreign Relations of the United States (F.R.U.S.):
Paris Peace Conference, 1919, Vols. III, VI, XII, XIII.
1925, Vol. I.
Soviet Union, 1933–39.
1941, Vol. I, General, The Soviet Union.
1942, Europe, Vol. III.
The Conferences at Cairo and Teheran, 1943.
The Conferences at Malta and Yalta, 1945.
The Conference of Berlin, 1945, 2 vols.

German Foreign Ministry Documents: this material, consisting of unpublished documents from the archives of the German Foreign Office during the Weimar Republic and the Third Reich, is at present available in photostat form in the Public Records Office and the Foreign Office Library. It is referred to here as GFM2 followed by the serial and frame number of the photostats.

Im Dunkel der europäischen Geheimdiplomatie. Iswolskis Kriegspolitik in Paris, 1911–17, Vol. II, ed. Stieve, Berlin, 1926.

Lokarnskaya Konferentsiya 1925 g., Dokumenti, ed. Dobrov *et al.*, Moscow, 1959.

Mezhdunarodniye Otnosheniya v epokhu Imperializma, Series III,
Vol. VI, Pts. I and II, Moscow/Leningrad, 1931.
Nazi-Soviet Relations, 1939–41 (N.S.R.), Washington, 1948.
New Documents on the history of Munich, Prague, 1958.

2. PARLIAMENTARY AND OTHER DEBATES

Documents of the Preparatory Commission of the Disarmament Con-
ference, Series V, Minutes of the 4th session; Series VIII, Minutes
of the 6th session, 1st Part.
International Military Tribunal, Trial of the Major War Criminals,
Vols. XXXIV, XXXVII, XL, Nuremberg, 1947.
Journal officiel, Débats parlementaires, No. 20, 1936.
Parliamentary Debates, House of Commons, Fifth Series, Vols. 100,
154, 181, 188, 194, 229, 281, 333, 345.
Protokolli: IX Syezda R.K.P. (b), Moscow, 1934.
X Syezda R.K.P. (b), Moscow, 1921.
XI Syezda R.K.P. (b), Moscow, 1936.
XIV Syezda R.K.P. (b), Moscow, 1926.
XV Konferentsii V.K.P. (b), Moscow, 1927.
Protokolli Zasedanii TsIK Sovetov: 2 Sozyv, 3 Sessiya, Moscow, 1935.
Verhandlungen des Reichstags, Vols. CCCXXX, CCCXLV, CCCXLVI,
CCCLI, CCCLII, CCCCXXVIII.

3. AUTOBIOGRAPHIES, BIOGRAPHIES, DIARIES,
MEMOIRS, ETC.

Assmann, K., Deutsche Schicksalsjahre, Wiesbaden, 1950.
Baker, R. S., Woodrow Wilson and World Settlement, 3 vols., London,
1923.
Bernadotte, Folke, The Fall of the Curtain, New York, 1945.
Blücher, W. von, Deutschlands Weg nach Rapallo, Wiesbaden, 1951.
Bryant, A., The Turn of the Tide, London, 1957.
Butler, J. R. M., Lord Lothian, London, 1960.
Byrnes, J., Speaking Frankly, London, 1947.
Callwell, S., Field-Marshal Sir Henry Wilson, Life and Letters, 2 vols.,
London, 1927.
Chamberlain, Sir A., Sundry Letters, Chamberlain Papers, University
of Birmingham Library.
Chapman-Huston, D., The Lost Historian, London, 1936.
Churchill, W. S., The Second World War, 6 vols., London, 1948–54.
Clay, H., Lord Norman, London, 1957.
Coulondre, R., De Staline à Hitler, Paris, 1950.
Curtius, J., Sechs Jahre Minister der Weimarer Republik, Heidelberg,
1948.

D'Abernon, Lord, *An Ambassador of Peace*, 3 vols., London, 1929-30.
The Eighteenth Decisive Battle of the World, London, 1931.
Davies, J., *Mission to Moscow*, London.
Deane, J. R., *The Strange Alliance*, London, 1947.
Dirksen, H. von, *Moscow-Tokyo-London*, Engl. trans., London, 1951.
Dodd, W. E. (ed.), *Ambassador Dodd's Diary 1933-1938*, London, 1941.
Dönitz, K., *Zehn Jahre und zwanzig Tage*, Bonn, 1958.
Ebert, F., *Schriften, Aufzeichnungen, Reden*, 2 vols., Dresden, 1926.
Eisenhower, D., *Crusade in Europe*, London, 1948.
Epstein, K., *Mathias Erzberger and the Dilemma of German Democracy*, Princeton, 1959.
Erzberger, M., *Erlebnisse im Weltkrieg*, Stuttgart/Berlin, 1920.
Feiling, K., *The Life of Neville Chamberlain*, London, 1946.
Flandin, P.-É., *Politique française 1919-1940*, Paris, 1947.
Foch, F., *Memoirs*, Engl. trans., London, 1931.
François-Poncet, A., *De Versailles à Potsdam*, Paris, 1948.
Gessler, O., *Reichswehrpolitik in der Weimarer Zeit*, ed. Sendtner, Stuttgart, 1958.
Hancock, K. W., *Smuts, the Sanguine Years 1870-1919*, Cambridge, 1962.
Helbig, H., *Die Träger der Rapallo-Politik*, Göttingen, 1958.
Herriot, É., *Jadis*, 2 vols., Paris, 1948-52.
Hilger, G., and Mayer, A., *The Incompatible Allies*, New York, 1953.
House, Col., *Intimate Papers*, 4 vols., ed. Seymour, London, 1928.
Hull, Cordell, *Memoirs*, 2 vols., New York, 1948.
Ironside Diaries 1937-1940, ed. R. Macleod and D. Kelly, London, 1962.
Jones, T. J., *A Diary with Letters 1931-1950*, Oxford, 1954.
Kirkpatrick, I., *The Inner Circle*, London, 1960.
Kleist, P., *Zwischen Hitler und Stalin*, Bonn, 1950.
Köller, K., *Der letzte Monat*, Mannheim, 1945.
Kordt, E., *Wahn und Wirklichkeit*, Stuttgart, 1947.
Krivitsky, W. G., *I was Stalin's Agent*, London, 1939.
Laroche, J., *La Pologne de Pilsudski*, Paris, 1953.
Leahy, W. D., *I was There*, London, 1950.
Leonhard, W., *Child of the Revolution*, Engl. trans., London, 1957.
Lloyd George, D., *War Memoirs*, 2 vols., London, 1938.
Lochner, L., *Herbert Hoover and Germany*, New York, 1960.
Lüdde-Neurath, W., *Regierung Dönitz*, Göttingen, 1951.
    Das Ende auf deutschem Boden (in *Bilanz des Zweiten Weltkriegs*, Oldenburg/Hamburg, 1953).
Mantoux, P., *Les Délibérations du Conseil des Quatre*, 2 vols., Paris, 1955.
Max von Baden, Prince, *Erinnerungen und Dokumente*, Berlin, 1927.
Montgomery, Field-Marshal, *Memoirs*, London, 1958.
Morgan, F., *Overture to Overlord*, London, 1950.

Morgan, J. H., *Assize of Arms*, I, London, 1945.
Mosely, Philip, *The Kremlin and World Politics*, New York, 1960.
Nadolny, R., *Mein Beitrag*, Wiesbaden, 1955.
Newton, Lord, *Lord Lansdowne*, London, 1929.
Papen, F. von, *Der Wahrheit eine Gasse*, Munich, 1952.
Paul-Boncour, J., *Entre deux guerres*, 3 vols., Paris, 1945–46.
Penrose, E. F., *Economic Planning for the Peace*, Princeton, 1953.
Petrie, Sir Charles, *Life and Letters of Austen Chamberlain*, 3 vols.,
    London, 1940.
Pingaud, A., *Histoire diplomatique de la France pendant la Grande
    Guerre*, 3 vols., Paris, 1937.
Rahn, R., *Ruheloses Leben*, Düsseldorf, 1950.
Reynaud, P., *La France a sauvé l'Europe*, 2 vols., Paris, 1947.
Ribbentrop, J. von, *Zwischen London und Moskau*, Leoni am Starn-
    berger See, 1953.
Ribot, A., *Journal*, Paris, 1936.
Scheidemann, Ph., *Der Zusammenbruch*, Berlin, 1921.
Schmidt, P., *Statist auf diplomatischer Bühne*, Bonn, 1950.
Schmidt-Pauli, Gen. von, *Seeckt*, Berlin, 1937.
Schultz, J., *Die letzten dreissig Tage*, Stuttgart, 1951.
Sherwood, R., *The White House Papers of Harry L. Hopkins*, 2 vols.,
    London, 1948.
Speidel, H. von, *We Defended Normandy*, Engl. trans., London,
    1951.
Stein, L., *Aus dem Leben eines Optimisten*, Berlin, 1930.
Stettinius, E., *Roosevelt and the Russians*, London, 1950.
Stockhausen, Max von, *Sechs Jahre Reichskanzlei*, Bonn, 1954.
Strang, Lord, *Home and Abroad*, London, 1956.
Stresemann, G., *Vermächtnis*, 3 vols., Berlin, 1932.
    Nachlass, Selected items, Public Records Office, London.
Stuart, Sir Campbell, *The Secrets of Crewe House*, London, 1920.
Suarez, G., *Briand—sa vie, son œuvre*, Vol. VI, Paris, 1952.
Templewood, Viscount, *Nine Troubled Years*, London, 1954.
Terrail, G. (Mermeix), *Les Négociations secrètes*, Vol. V, *Fragments
    d'histoire*, 1914–19, Paris, 1919.
Trotsky, L., *Von der Oktober Revolution bis zum Brester Frieden*,
    Berlin (n.d.).
Truman, H., *Year of Decisions, 1945*, London, 1955.
Webb, Beatrice, *Diaries 1912–1924*, ed. Margaret Cole, London,
    1952.
Weizsäcker, E. von, *Erinnerungen*, Munich, 1950.
Welles, Sumner, *The Time for Decision*, New York, 1944.
Whitaker, J. T., *We Cannot Escape History*, New York, 1943.
Young, G. M., *Stanley Baldwin*, London, 1952.
Zetkin, K., *Erinnerungen an Lenin*, Vienna, 1929.

4. PAMPHLETS AND COLLECTIONS OF SPEECHES, ETC.

Chicherin, G. V. (1) *Foreign Policy of Soviet Russia—Report of Narko-mindel to 7th All-Russian Congress of Soviets*, Engl. trans., London, 1920.
(2) *An die deutschen Arbeiter*, Moscow, 1919.
(3) *Vnyeshnyaya Politika Sovietskoi Rossii za dva goda*, Moscow, 1920.
Hitler's Speeches, ed. Baynes, N. H., 2 vols., Oxford, 1942.
Lenin, V. I., *Sochineniya*, Vols. XXVIII, XXX, XXXI (4th ed.).
Litvinov, M., *Vnyeshnyaya Politika SSSR*, Moscow, 1937.
Maisky, I., *Vnyeshnyaya Politika RSFRS*, *1917–1922*, Moscow, 1922.
Molotov, V., *V Borbe za Sotzialism*, Moscow, 1935.
Poincaré, R., *Histoire politique—Chroniques de Quinzaine*, IV, Paris, 1922.
Radek, K., *Zur Taktik des Kommunismus*, Berlin, 1919.
'Die auswärtige Politik des deutschen Kommunismus und der Hamburger National-Bolschewismus', *Die Internationale 17–18*, December 20, 1919.
'Die auswärtige Politik Sowjet-Russlands', Hamburg, 1921 (written December 1919).
'Deutschland und Russland', *Die Zukunft*, No. 19, February 7th, 1920.
The Winding up of the Versailles Treaty, Engl. trans., Hamburg, 1922.
'Noyabr', *Krasnaya Nov*, October 1926.
Rakovsky, Kh., *Liga Natsii i SSSR*, Moscow, 1926.
Rathenau, W., *Cannes und Genua*, Berlin, 1922.
Stalin, J., *Leninism*, II, Engl. trans., London, 1933.
Report to 17th Congress of C.P.S.U. (b), Moscow, 1951.
The Great Patriotic War of the Soviet Union, New York, 1945.
Stresemann, G., *Essays and Speeches on Various Subjects*, Engl. trans., London, 1930.

5. THE PRESS

Bulletin of International News
Soviet Russia
The Observer
The Scotsman
The Times
Bolshevik
Izvestiya
Mezhdunarodnaya Zhizn
Pravda
Voina i Rabochii Klass

6. Miscellaneous Articles

Beloff, M., 'Soviet Foreign Policy 1929–1941: Some Notes', *Soviet Studies*, II/2 1951.

Birke, E., 'Die französische Osteuropapolitik 1914–1918', *Zeitschrift für Ostforschung*, III/3, 1954.

Cambon, J., 'La Paix—notes inédites 1919', *Revue de Paris*, November 1st, 1937.

Carsten, F. L., 'The Reichswehr and the Red Army', *Survey*, No. 44-5, October, 1962.

Dorn, W., 'The Debate on American Occupation Policy in Germany 1944–1945', *Political Science Quarterly*, LXXII, December 1957.

Epstein, F. T., 'Zur Interpretation des Versailler Vertrags', *Jahrbücher für Geschichte Osteuropas*, V/3, 1957.

Erdmann, K. D., 'Das Problem der Ost- oder Westorientierung in der Locarno-Politik Stresemanns', *Geschichte in Wissenschaft und Unterricht*, VI/3, March 1955.

Gasiorowski, Z., 'The Russian Overture to Germany of December 1924', *Journal of Modern History*, XXX, No. 2, June 1958.

'Stresemann and Poland before Locarno', *Journal of Central European Affairs*, XVIII, No. I, April, 1958.

'Stresemann and Poland after Locarno', *Journal of Central European Affairs*, XVIII, No. 3, October, 1958.

Gatzke, H. W. 'Russo-German Military Collaboration During the Weimar Republic', *American Historical Review*, LXIII, No. 3, April 1958.

Hirsch, E. F., 'Stresemann in Historical Perspective', *Review of Politics*, XV, No. 3, July, 1953.

Korsunski, A., 'Rapallski Dogovor i Nemetskaya Sotzial-Demokratiya', *Voprosi Istorii*, No. 8, 1950.

Maehl, W., 'The German Socialists and the Foreign Policy of the Reich from the London Conference to Rapallo', *Journal of Modern History*, No. 1, March 1947.

Rosenfeld, G., 'Das Zustandekommen des Rapallo-Vertrags', *Zeitschrift für Geschichtswissenschaft*, IV/4, 1956.

Speidel, H. von, 'Reichswehr und Rote Armee', *Vierteljahrshefte fur Zeitgeschichte*, I/1, January 1953.

Thimme, A., 'Die Locarno-Politik im Lichte des Stresemannschen Nachlasses', *Zeitschrift für Politik*, III/1, 1956.

Tsitovitch, Ya., 'O roli S.Sh.A. v spasenii Germanii ot polnovo razgroma v 1918 godu', *Voprosi Istorii*, No. 12, 1950.

Wallace, W. V., 'The Foreign Policy of President Beneš in its Approach to Munich', *Slavonic and East European Review*, Vol. 39, 1960-61.

7. OTHER WORKS REFERRED TO

Beloff, M., *The Foreign Policy of Soviet Russia 1929–1941*, 2 vols., Oxford, 1947–49.

Bergmann, C., *The History of Reparations*, Engl. trans., London, 1927.

Carr, E. H., *Russo-German Relations between the two World Wars*, Johns Hopkins, 1952.

Churchill, W. S., *The World Crisis—The Aftermath*, London, 1929.

Deborin, G. A., *Vtoraya Mirovaya Voina—Voenno-Politicheskii Ocherk*, Moscow, 1958.

Duroselle, J.-B., *et al.*, *Les Relations germano-soviétiques 1933–1939*, Paris, 1954.

Ehrman, J., *Grand Strategy*, Vol. VI, London, 1956.

Feis, H., *Churchill, Roosevelt, Stalin*, Oxford, 1957.

Fischer, Fritz, *Griff nach der Weltmacht*, Düsseldorf, 1962.

Fischer, L., *The Soviets in World Affairs*, 2 vols., London, 1930.

Freund, G., *The Unholy Alliance*, London, 1957.

Hancock, W. K., *War and Peace in this Century*, Cambridge, 1961.

Headlam-Morley, Sir James, *Studies in Diplomatic History*, London, 1930.

History of The Times, Vol. IV, Part I, London, 1952.

Höltje, Ch., *Die Weimarer Republik und das Ost-Locarno Problem 1919–1934*, Würzburg, 1958.

Hölzle, E., *Der Osten im ersten Weltkrieg*, Leipzig, 1944.

Israelyan, V. L., *Diplomaticheskaya Istoriya Velikoi Otechestvennoi Voini*, Moscow, 1959.

Ivanov, L. N., *Ocherki Mezhdunarodnikh Otnoshenii v Period Vtoroi Mirovoi Voini*, Moscow, 1958.

Koblyakov, I. K., *Ot Bresta do Rapallo*, Moscow, 1954.

Kochan, L., *Russia and the Weimar Republic*, Cambridge, 1954.

Langer, W. L., and Gleason, S. E., *Challenge to Isolation*, London, 1952.

Lloyd, Lord, *The British Case*, London, 1939.

McInnis, E., *et al.*, *The Shaping of Post-war Germany*, London, 1960.

Meinck, G., *Hitler und die deutsche Aufrüstung*, Wiesbaden, 1959.

Micaud, Ch., *The French Right and Nazi Germany*, Durham (U.S.), 1943.

Namier, L. B., *Conflicts*, London, 1942.

Ocherki Istorii Velikoi Otechestvennoi Voini 1941–1945, Moscow, 1955.

Pogue, F. C., *The Supreme Command*, Washington, 1954.

Pospelov, P. N. (ed.), *Istoriya Velikoi Otechestvennoi Voini Sovetskovo Soyuza*, I, Moscow, 1960.

Ritter, G., *Carl Goerdeler und die deutsche Widerstandsbewegung*, Stuttgart, 1954.

Rothfels, H., *Bismarck und der Staat*, Stuttgart, 1955.
Rozek, E. J., *Allied Wartime Diplomacy*, New York, 1958.
Sarkissian, A. O., ed., *Studies in Diplomatic History*, London, 1961.
Schieder, Th., *Die Probleme des Rapallo-Vertrags*, Cologne, 1956.
Seeckt, H. von, *Deutschland zwischen Ost und West*, Hamburg, 1933.
Selsam, J. P., *The Attempts to form an Anglo-French Alliance 1919–
    1929*, Philadelphia, 1936.
Snell, J. L., *Wartime Origins of the East-West Dilemma over Germany*,
    New Orleans, 1959.
Stein, B. E., *Russkii Vopros v 1920–1921 gg.*, Moscow, 1958.
Stern, Leo (ed.), *Die Probleme der Geschichte des Zweiten Weltkriegs*,
    Berlin, 1958.
Tanin, M., *Desyat Let Vnyeshnei Politiki SSSR 1917–1927*, Moscow,
    1927.
Tansill, Ch., *Back Door to War*, Chicago, 1952.
The World in March 1939, Oxford.
Turok, V. M., *Lokarno, Moscow/Leningrad*, 1949.
Wandycz, P. S., *France and her Eastern Allies, 1919-1925*, Minnea-
    polis, 1962.
Wheeler-Bennett, J. W., *The Nemesis of Power*, London, 1953.
Wilmot, C., *The Struggle for Europe*, London, 1952.
Woodward, Sir Llewellyn, *British Foreign Policy in the Second World
    War*, London, 1962.
Zimmermann, L., *Deutsche Aussenpolitik in der Ära der Weimarer
    Republik*, Göttingen, 1958.
Zitelmann, F. C., *Russland im Friedensvertrage von Versailles*, Berlin,
    1920.

INDEX